WHAT PEOPLE AR[

PAGAN PORT/

This book is a confident piece of work that is both erudite and lucid – no easy task at any time, but when handling such a complex and sensitive subject it is extremely difficult. Not only does this book succeed, it seems to me to be a model to which other writers should aspire. Its clarity and the author's obvious enthusiasm for the subject make it a compelling read. An excellent compendium of the subject worth its place on anyone's shelf.

Graeme K Talboys, author of *The Way of the Druid*

Pagan Portals – Brigid: Meeting the Celtic Goddess of Poetry, Forge, and Healing Well is one of the best introductions to Brigid that I have read. The book is well researched and grounded in mythology and folklore, offering the reader a thorough overview of the Goddess as well as dealing with popular misconceptions. I particularly appreciated the inclusion of the lesser known Irish Brigids, the author's own experiences and her suggestions for further exploration. Daimler's style of writing, with her blend of the scholarly and the personal, ensures that the book is accessible and of interest to beginners and more experienced pagans. I would highly recommend this book to those seeking to connect with Brigid.

Jane Brideson, artist and blogger at The Ever-Living Ones – Irish Goddesses & Gods in landscape, myth & custom

Brigid is a complex figure whose worship has transcended place, making her one of the few truly pan-Celtic deities; transcended traditions, as she is believed to have survived into the Christian period as the beloved St. Brigid; and transcended time, as she continues to inspire Pagans and Christians alike into the present day. It is no wonder that there is a complex body of lore that has woven itself around Brigid, and many books have been written to explore the different strands of tradition that surround her both as Goddess and as saint. In this work, Morgen Daimler deftly distills various streams of information into a short, well-researched book that presents the lore as it is found in primary source materials, discusses traditional folk practices from various Celtic lands, and shares her personal experiences as a devotee of Brigid. An excellent resource, *Pagan Portals – Brigid: Meeting the Celtic Goddess of Poetry, Forge, and Healing Well* provides a grounded foundation for anyone who feels called to work with Brigid, and is an excellent, fact-based starting point for further research.

Jhenah Telyndru (MA, Celtic Studies), author of *Avalon Within: A Sacred Journey of Myth, Mystery and Inner Wisdom*

Morgan Daimler has written another accessible and scholarly book in the Moon Books Pagan Portals series, this time on the Goddess Brigid. It allows the reader with little previous exposure to Celtic Polytheism to begin worshiping Brigid in ways that are traditional, practical, and relevant. To devotees of Brigid, the book is a practical little gem, a summary of much they know, and probably quite a bit they don't. To devotees of other deities, the book serves as an introduction to one of the most popular of Goddesses. In short, I can't recommend it highly enough.

Segomâros Widugeni, formerly Aedh Rua, author of *Celtic Flame*

In *Pagan Portals – Brigid*, Morgan Daimler brings us an exciting and superbly researched introduction to the pan-Celtic Goddess Brigid. Combining history and lore from all major Celtic mythologies with personal experiences and observations, the author brings us before the Goddess feeling as though we have already been introduced and welcomed into Her realm. The many names, stories, animals, plants, holidays and lore of the Goddess are all given to us enlivened by the author's encounters with Brigid. She rounds off the book with a brief look at the Goddess in today's world and gives us some prayers, chants, charms and rituals to consider for our own workings with this inspirational Goddess of Poetry, Healing and the Forge. You couldn't ask for a finer introduction to this most enchanting of Goddesses.

Gary and **Ruth Colcombe**, the Celtic Myth Podshow

Morgan Daimler's work on Brigid is fresh yet thoroughly rooted in the legends and lore. The readable style captures the complexity that is this once-and-future Goddess. Morgan gets Brigid – not as a shadow or an archetype but as a fully-fledged Being. Highly recommended.

H. Byron Ballard, author of *Asfidity and Mad-Stones*

I always look forward to a new book from Morgan Daimler. Her research is solid, her writing is clear, and her concise work gets to the heart of the matter quickly. I couldn't ask for a better intro-duction to Brigid as a Goddess. Even after my two decades of Brigidine flamekeeping, I learned new things from this brief book. Highly recommended!

Erynn Rowan Laurie, author of *Ogam: Weaving Word Wisdom*

Pagan Portals
Brigid

Meeting the Celtic Goddess of Poetry, Forge,
and Healing Well

Pagan Portals
Brigid

Meeting the Celtic Goddess of Poetry, Forge,
and Healing Well

Morgan Daimler

Winchester, UK
Washington, USA

First published by Moon Books, 2016
Moon Books is an imprint of John Hunt Publishing Ltd., Laurel House, Station Approach,
Alresford, Hants, SO24 9JH, UK
office1@jhpbooks.net
www.johnhuntpublishing.com
www.moon-books.net

For distributor details and how to order please visit the 'Ordering' section on our website.

Text copyright: Morgan Daimler 2015

ISBN: 978 1 78535 320 8
Library of Congress Control Number: 2015953280

A CIP catalogue record for this book is available from the British Library.

Design: Lee Nash
Cover Art "Brigid of the Forge" copyright Ashley Bryner.

Printed and bound by CPI Group (UK) Ltd, Croydon, CR0 4YY

We operate a distinctive and ethical publishing philosophy in all
areas of our business, from our global network of authors to
production and worldwide distribution.

CONTENTS

Acknowledgements xii

Author's Note xiii

Introduction 1

Chapter One: Meeting Brigid 3

Chapter Two: Brigid by Other Names 15

Chapter Three: Brigid in Mythology 25

Chapter Four: Symbols, Animals, and Holidays 37

Chapter Five: The Goddess in Modern Times 53

Chapter Six: Prayers, Chants and Charms 63

Conclusion 73

Appendix A: Pronunciation 75

Appendix B: Mixed Media Resources 77

Bibliography 80

Endnotes 83

This book is dedicated to my daughter Amara, who has had a special love for Brighid since she was old enough to say the Goddess's name. You asked me when I wrote the Morrigan book to write you one about Brighid – here it is Mari, I hope you like it.

Acknowledgements

I'd like to thank Patty Taylor for responding on my Facebook author page and suggesting the idea of more Pagan Portals focused on different Goddesses, and my editor with Moon Books, Trevor Greenfield, for asking if I'd be interested in this project. Without both of those things happening and coming together this book wouldn't be here today.

Also a huge thank you to Segomâros Widugeni for help with the Gaulish pronunciations. You are truly an invaluable resource to the Reconstructionist community.

And most of all, with thanks to Brighid, Lady of the Smith's Forge, Lady of the Healing Well, Lady of the Poet's Harp. I didn't know when I chose to step into that ritual circle and face you what would come of it, but I am profoundly grateful that I did it. May this book be my offering to you, in gratitude for your gifts to me. Trebrech faelte, a Brig, i mu bethu. Do beannacht form, mo láes dait. Indossa ocus co dé mbrátha.

Author's Note

Brigid is one of the most popular Celtic Goddesses today and there are a variety of resources available to learn about her. Many of them discuss both the pagan Goddess Brigid and the Irish saint, understandable since the division between the two beings is fluid at best. Others focus largely or entirely on Brigid in a modern context and incorporate a lot of the author's personal views and experiences. *Pagan Portals: Brigid* was written as a resource for seekers of the pagan Goddess specifically and offers both solid academic material and anecdotes of connecting with Brigid in a format that is accessible and designed to be easy to read. It is meant to be a basic introduction to this Goddess and also a bridge for beginners to feel more comfortable with the longer more in-depth books available on the market, allowing a reader to get a thorough grounding in Brigid's lore before moving forward.

In writing this I have drawn on many different sources and have carefully referenced and cited all of them. My own degree is in psychology so I prefer to use the APA (American Psychological Association) method of citations. This means that within the text after quotes or paraphrased material the reader will see a set of parenthesis containing the author's last name and date the source was published; this can then be cross references with the bibliography at the end of the book. I find this method to be a good one and I prefer it over footnotes or other methods of citation, which is why it's the one I use.

While this book can and does serve as a stand-alone work, ideally I hope that the reader will be drawn to learn more and decide to continue seeking. Brigid is a complex deity and no single book, of any length, can entirely capture her layers and depth. To help readers use this book as a stepping stone towards further connection I have provided a list of both the references I used in my writing and also of recommended further reading at the end of the book under the bibliography. I have tried to offer books that represent an array of options for people, with different viewpoints and approaches to honoring Brigid.

As I have said before in my previous book, *Pagan Portals: The Morrigan*, I do not think that the religious framework we use to connect to the Gods matters as much as the effort to honor the old Gods itself. I think we can all do this respectfully and with an appreciation for history without the need for any particular religion. Whether we are Reconstructionists, Wiccans, or Celtic pagans, all that really matter is that we are approaching our faith with sincerity and a genuine intention. To that end this book is written without any specific spiritual faith in mind, beyond polytheism, and it is up to the reader to decide how best to incorporate the material. My own personal path is Irish Reconstructionist Polytheism so that is bound to color some of my opinions in the text, however, and the reader may want to keep that in mind.

I have been an Irish pagan since 1991 and have long included Brigid in my worship as a Goddess of healing, and also Brigid as a Goddess of poetry. Although she is not one of the primary Goddesses I honor she is an important one, and in each chapter I am going to include a little section on my own personal experiences with her. For some people this book may be the first step in a life-long journey, the first attempt to reach out to this important and complex Goddess. For others this book may simply provide a greater understanding of the Goddess, her history, and modern beliefs and practices associated with her. In either case I hope that the reader feels that some value is gained from the time spent with this little volume, getting to know Brigid.

Morgan Daimler, September 21st, 2015

Introduction

The Celtic Gods have always seemed to hold a special fascination for many modern pagans, and several in particular have become quite well known. Perhaps the best example of this is Brigid, who has found a place in many people's hearts and on their altars. As she has gained in modern popularity her stories – her history and myth – have become increasingly shrouded in obscurity and her origins have started to blur and blend with romanticism until the truth can be hard to decipher. A creation story featuring Brigid as the main force pushing the Irish Gods to make the world, which sprung from the creative imaginings of an Irish poet at the turn of the 20th century, is now often taken as ancient belief, while the myth of Brigid as the wife of a king of the Tuatha Dé Danann falls into obscurity. Another creation story, written within the past 20 years and pairing Brigid romantically with a God usually said to be her father, has also become immensely popular and is shared as historically pagan, while her place as a Goddess of outlaws and the displaced remains little known. The lore of the Catholic saint is attributed to the pagan Goddess, and some people see shadows of the Goddess in the saint. For many people new to Brigid, or to studying Celtic or Irish mythology, it can be extremely confusing to try to sort the old beliefs from the modern, to tell the Irish from the Scottish. The end result is that some people who are drawn to honor the Goddess Brigid find themselves lost in a seemingly endless assortment of possibilities. Brigid's mythology forms an enormous, brightly colored tapestry and it can be easy to get so overwhelmed by the larger picture that we lose the small details; this book is intended to help guide a seeker in understanding who Brigid was, and is, so that both the beauty of the picture and the intricacy of the details can be appreciated.

The information we have relating to Brigid comes from the

traditional mythology including the *Cath Maige Tuired* and *Lebor Gabala Erenn* as well as mythology of the Christian saint of the same name who many believe is a continuation of the Goddess; modern beliefs and practices surrounding Brigid are an amalgam of older pagan sources and newer Christian ones. Much of this is due to the logical assumption that many of the beliefs and practices surrounding the saint reflect older pre-Christian beliefs originally attached to the Goddess. By studying the myth and folklore we can gain valuable insight into who Brigid was in order to understand her roots in the pagan culture and her renewal in modern culture. She also has a very complex bridge between the two as a Catholic saint, but that will be touched on only very briefly in this book, which seeks to explore primarily the pagan material relating the Goddess.[1]

The 9th century text *Cormac's Glossary* says that 'almost all Irish Goddesses are called a Brigit' (Sanas Cormaic, n.d.). Of course most if not all Irish deity names are actually titles or epithet so it's hard to judge how meaningful that was in the pagan period, but it does confirm Brigid's significance. The Old Irish word Bríg means: power, force, might strength, vigor, virtue, and authority (Quin, 1983). O'hOgáin believes Brigid's name means 'exalted one', similar to the meaning given to the related British Goddess Brigantia of 'high one' (O'hOgáin, 2006; Ross, 1970). So the very meaning of her name reinforces the idea that she was a Goddess of primary importance, a deity who filled a variety of roles, from fostering new lives to keening for the dead, from supporting the landless warriors at the edges of society to upholding the right order of the world. Brigid was truly, and perhaps more so than any other deity, a Goddess for all people.

Chapter One

Meeting Brigid

Trí aithgine in domain: brú mná, uth bó, ness gobann.
Traditional Irish Triad

Three regenerators of the world: a woman's womb, a cow's udder, a smith's furnace. (Translation, M. Daimler)

One of the most popular Irish Goddesses in modern times is Brigid, known as both a pagan Goddess and for her associations with the later Catholic saint of the same name. A pan-Celtic Goddess, Brigid is found across a variety of Celtic cultures;[2] in Ireland (in Irish) she is Bríd, or Brighid, which has been Anglicized to Bridgid or Bridgit; In Scotland she is Bride and in Wales she is Ffraid. In Old Irish her name was Brig or Bric, in Middle Irish she was Brigit, while in Celtic Britain she was Brigantia, and in Gaul she was Brigandu.

In Ireland Brigid was a deity of healing, poetry and smithcraft, sometimes seen as a single deity and sometimes as three sister deities. As three sisters, they were: Brigid of the Poets, Brigid of the Forge, and Brigid the Healer. It is very difficult, however, to sort out which Brigid of the three was the one indicated in most of the stories or references to her. Many people simply treat her as a single Goddess, although this may be oversimplifying. For a modern polytheist who wants to honor all three Brigids, logical choices must be made about which Brigid would have most fit each story or attribution; that said Brigid here will be discussed as a single Goddess, with the understanding that any one of the three could likely be referred to. Additionally there are several other Irish Brigids: Brig Ambue (Brigid of the Cowless), Brig Brethach (Brigid of the Judgments), and Brig Brigiu (Brigid the

Hospitaller). These three may be later interpretations of the previous three – and indeed Irish scholar Kim McCone describes them as such – or they may be different Goddesses, or perhaps even different aspects of a single Brigid. It is up to the reader to decide for themselves what view makes the most sense, but information about all of the named Brigids will be given below.

Relationships

Finding anything clear cut in Irish myth is difficult and this is true of trying to sort out Brigid's genealogy. Brigid's mother is not listed, and in the material we have she is simply called the daughter of the Dagda, or daughters of the Dagda since she also appears as three identically named siblings. Brigid is sometimes conflated with Danu, and less often with the Morrigan, because of instances in the *Lebor Gabala Erenn* where each is said to be the mother to the same set of three sons by the same father. It is impossible to know with certainty if this is so, or only a medieval attempt to reconcile the pagan mythology into a more cohesive system, and so some people accept it and some people don't. However, it is worth noting that Danu and the Morrigan have a different father than Brigid does, a fact which is mentioned repeatedly, making it unlikely in my opinion that they actually are the same being.[3]

In mythology she was married to the half-Fomorian, half-Tuatha Dé Danann Eochaid Bres and bore him a son Ruadán.[4] In some stories she also had three sons with Tuireann named Brian, Iachar, and Iucharba although this may result from confusion between her and Danu/Danand who is listed as the mother of these three sons elsewhere. This confusion is reinforced by other sources, which list Brian, Iachar, and Iucharba as either sons of Brigid and Bres or sons of Bres (Gray, 1983). No daughters are attributed to her, and all of her sons die tragically by violence: Ruadán is killed after a failed assassination attempt of the smith God Goibniu during the war with the Fomorians and Brian,

Iachar, and Iucharba die after completing a series of nearly impossibly tasks set by the high king Lugh as punishment for killing his father.

She is viewed as the sister of Angus mac Og, which plays an important role in some of the recent stories surrounding Imbolc, Brigid's special holiday. As a daughter of the Dagda she would also have had at least two other brothers, Aed, and Cermait, according to the *Lebor Gabala Erenn* (Macalister, 1941).

Associations

Brigid is a protector and inspirer of poets, as well as being connected to agricultural fertility and healing (O'hOgain, 2006; Clark, 1991). As a Goddess of poets she would also have had ties to prophecy, a skill practiced by the Irish poets and considered essential to their art. Nerys Patterson describes her as 'the high goddess Brig, patron of food production, war, and knowledge' (Patterson, 1994). Brigid is sometimes equated with the Roman Minerva as a Goddess of healing and skill and the Greek Athena (Green1995; McNeil1956). She was said to have two oxen, a pig, and a ram who were all the kings of their respective species, which could further relate her to domestic animals, and in folk tradition she is regularly called on as saint Brigid to heal animals. Brigid has many strong associations to healing, both of animals and people, and also to protection and blessing in folk magic charms as can be seen in the *Carmina Gadelica* material. Her healing of people is both general and specific to women, who prayed to her to conceive, during pregnancy, labor, and also for issues such as mastitis. In Scotland Brigid as Bride is strongly associated with childbirth; it is said that if a woman has an easy birth Brigid is with her, but a difficult birth means Brigid does not favor the family (Ross, 1976).

She is also seen as a Goddess of prosperity and abundance who blesses homes she visits (Sjoestedt, 1940). As the tutelary Goddess of Leinster she could arguable be seen as a sovereignty deity as well; her marriage to one of the kings of the Tuatha Dé Danann, Bres, would reinforce this idea as the kings of the Gods were each associated in some way with a particular sovereignty Goddess.[5] A poem in the *Lebar na Núachongbála* calls Brigid the Lady of Sovereignty, further confirming this association (Meyer, 1912).

Many people see her as a mother Goddess; the saint is referred to as the foster mother of Christ and this may well reflect an older feeling that Brigid was motherly to all those who prayed to her or honored her. Celtic scholar Anne Ross associates Brigid with the role of mother of the Gods, comparing her to Danu and to the Welsh Dôn, and groups them as deities who are 'gods of the divinities themselves', or in other words deities who the Gods themselves would go to in the same way people went to the Gods (Ross, 1970). Professor Marie-Louise Sjoestedt, a linguist who wrote about Celtic mythology and themes, refers to Brigid as a 'goddess par excellence' along with Danu and Anu and writes that 'the pagan Brigit was the most excellent goddess' (Sjoestedt, 1940, p. 25). In some sources including the *Lebor Gabala Erenn* Brigid is conflated with both Danu and the Morrigan, which is sometimes used to support the viewpoint of her as a mother Goddess or even as the mother of the Gods, although the confusion between the three Goddesses might only be a result of later attempts to homogenize different local folklore into a single mythological system. In this view Ross argues that Brigid is ultimately an earth-mother Goddess who supports and nurtures the Gods themselves and who is the mother of exceptional children, whose skill exceeds the other Gods (Ross, 1970). Certainly Brigid does have an unusually broad range of abilities and expertise, which at least indicates that she held a significant and prominent place historically.

Brigid has tenuous war aspects in Ireland, although thinly disguised as saint Brigid. Lady Gregory in her book *Gods and Fighting Men* sought to chronicle Irish folk beliefs in the 19th century and related a story of the battle of Dunbolg, which saw the war Goddess Badb, one of the Morrigans, aligning with one army while Brigid incited the other army (Clark, 1991). In one version of this tale Brigid simply looms over the Leinstermen, the side she favors, intimidating the enemy, but in another version she takes an active part in frightening them so that they are defeated (O Cathasaigh, 2014). In this tale we can fairly easily see the tutelary Goddesses of Leinster and Connacht facing off in Brigid's and Badb's support of the army from their respective territory. One aspect of Brigid in particular, Brigid Ambue, who will be discussed in detail below, is strongly associated with the landless wandering warriors and the Irish style of warfare typified by cattle raiding, adding another connection between Brigid and war.

In Wales we also see Brigid, as the Welsh saint Ffraid, associated with beer and brewing, an association shared with her Irish counterpart (Baring-Gould, & Fisher, 1913). Saint Brigid was reputed to be the best brewer in Ireland, and her association with beer, ale, and brewing were shared by her counterparts in Scotland, saint Bride, as well as the Welsh Ffraid. This particular association may reflect an older pagan belief connected to Brigid of Smithcraft, as it was not uncommon for smith deities to also be Gods of brewing. The Irish smith God Goibniu, for example, was associated with brewing as well as smithing. Goibniu had a special mead or ale called the fled Goibnenn, 'drink of Goibniu', that conveyed the gift of youth and immortality to the Tuatha De Danann (O hOgain, 2006). Similarly the Welsh Gofannon was a brewer as well as smith and the Gaulish Secullos, the 'Good Striker', although not known explicitly as a smith God was depicted with a hammer and associated with wine. The process of brewing itself is one which, like blacksmithing, involves using both fire and water to transform a substance;[6] this may be particularly appropriate for a Goddess like Brigid who has such strong associations to fire and water, and it should be noted in connecting Brigid to brewing that one type of wheat used in making malt, emmer, is also one possible meaning of Brigid's son Rúadán's name.

The Many Brigids: Triplicities of the Goddess

In Irish mythology it was common to see significant deities appear in groups or as multiplicities of deities with the same name (Macalister, 1941). There are at least two distinct groupings of three Brigids. The first is a set of three sisters, all daughters of the Dagda, each of which is given a specific focus. The second trio is mentioned in the *Ulster Cycle* in relation to Senchan the chief poet and judge of the Ulster court: Brigid the Hospitaller (Brig Brigiu) is his mother, Brigid of the Judgments (Brig Brethach) is his wife, and their daughter is Brigid of the Cowless (Brig Ambue) (Thompson, 2014). Within this second grouping, however, each of the three Brigids is often mentioned inter-changeably and the epithet of one may be applied in a story to another, creating confusion, and implying the possibility of an older belief that perhaps the three were originally one cohesive figure only later divided. For some people the variety of Brigids in the different myths and stories will be seen as unique individuals and not all may be perceived as deities while to others each of these appearances of Brigid reflects a deeper united divine nature. It is up to the reader to decide for themselves, but the various evidence will be presented here.

The Three Sisters

Brigit – a poet, daughter of the Dagda. This Brigit is a woman of poetry (female poet) and is Brigit the Goddess worshipped by poets because her protection was very great and well known. This is why she is called a Goddess by poets. Her sisters were Brigit the woman of healing and Brigit the woman of smithcraft, Goddesses; they are three daughters of the Dagda.
(Daimler, 2015)

Brigid of the Poets

Besides her connection to fertility and domestic animals she is also strongly associated with poetry as well as several vocal expressions from warning cries to grieving (Ellis, 1994; Gray, 1983). The associations with warning cries come from her possession of the animals which cried out in times of social upheaval, and with her invention of a whistle to signal at night. Because of the incident in the *Cath Maige Tuired* where her son Ruadán is killed, she is said to be the first to ever grieve and keen (caoin) in Ireland, although the Dindshenchas tradition says she began the practice to mourn the death of Mac Greine (Gray, 1983). It should be noted here that Mac Greine, a later king of the Tuatha De Danann, would have been her nephew, her brother Cermait's son. Her connection to different types of vocal expression is strong and repeatedly emphasized throughout her stories.

Brigid of Healing

Listed in *Cormac's Glossary* as a sister of Brigid the Poetess, we are told only that she is a 'woman of healing'. The ancient sources for her in this role are scant, but in modern folk magic Brigid is one of the main beings called on for healing purposes. She is strongly associated with childbirth, called on during the birth itself and also to bless the child afterwards, and she is also called on for healing animals.

Brigid of Smithcraft

In *Cormac's Glossary* she is listed as the third Brigid, also a daughter of the Dagda. We are told that she is a 'woman of smithcraft' and explicitly that she is a Goddess, but nothing else. It is likely that this aspect of Brigid may relate to Brigid as a fire Goddess, as fire was an essential element of the smith's craft. It is generally taken as inarguable that Brigid was a Goddess of fire and possibly also of the sun (McCone, 2000).

The Three Brigids of the Ulster Cycle

Brigid the Hospitaller
Brigid the Hospitaller is associated with providing hospitality to those seeking it. The word 'brigiu' is used in old Irish legal texts to denote wealthy land owners who had to provide food and shelter in the manner of a hostel, whose honor price was equal to a king's, and who often served as mediators or judges in disputes (eDIL, n.d.). Through this aspect we may see Brigid associated with generosity and hospitality. It is also worth noting that hostels in mythology were often Otherworldly in nature or location and the people who kept them, the hospitallers, were often magical in nature (Lehmann, & Lehmann, 1975). There seems to be a clear connection between this Brigid in particular and the earliest depictions of saint Brigid who was renowned for miraculously being able to provision people with supplies, food, and drink (McCone, 2000). This aspect of Brigid as a provider of resources and nurturer could be correlated above with Brigid of Healing (McCone, 2000). Both provide nurturing and support of the physical body.

Brigid of the Judgments
Brigid the judge is a figure who appears in the *Ulster Cycle* and is referenced in the Brehon Laws. Although she appears as a semi-historic figure in the Ulster stories it is quite likely in my opinion that this Brigid was originally viewed as a deity, possibly identical with Brigid the Poetess. In one story of Brigid of the Judgments, a false judgment was given in a ruling about women resulting in blisters on the face of the judge who spoke; these were only cured when Brigid spoke the correct judgment (Kelly, 1988). In the *Ulster Cycle* her husband is one of the foster-fathers of Cu Chulain implying that she could possibly have been the hero's foster mother, a logical conclusion given the more general association of Brigid with the role of foster-mothering

(Thompson, 2014). Brigid of the Judgments could be associated with Brigid of the Poets (McCone, 2000). Both are connected to the power of speech.

Brigid of the Cowless

Brig Ambue is an obscure figure from the *Ulster Cycle*. Her father is the chief poet and judge of Ulster and her mother is Brigid of the Judgments (Thompson, 2014). This Brigid, like her parents, is associated with legal judgment, but is also seen as a patroness of both women and the lowest classes of people who she rendered judgments for in legal cases (Thompson, 2014). Brigid of the Cowless tends to be strongly associated with warriors, particularly those on the fringes of society. The word 'ambue' in Old Irish literally means 'no cows' and was a term used to classify people without property, land, or family, as well as foreigners (eDIL, n.d.). The ambue, or cowless, were generally young, unmarried warriors and hunters who lived on the edges of society, particularly being associated with the warrior bands called the fían (McCone, 2000). The warrior bands had their own structures and yearly cycles, tending to form during summer months during periods with lower agricultural activity (Patterson, 1994). It is interesting to contemplate Brigid of the Cowless and how she may relate to the pagan Goddess Brigid who lost all four of her sons to violence after their own lawless actions brought fatal retribution back on them. Brigid Ambue could be associated with Brigid of Smithcraft (McCone, 2000). Both are connected in different ways to warriors.

Brigid in My Life

My first visible experience of Brigid in my life was not one I expected. I had been honoring her for many years, praying to her, making offerings, celebrating her on Oimelc (Imbolc). But I had never truly felt her presence before, except perhaps as a distant sensation of calm and comfort.

One year I had decided to attend a public chant circle being put on by Kellianna, a pagan folk singer, in honor of Imbolc. I had been to many other chant circles at this point and always enjoyed them; they were structured like loose neopagan rituals with group singing and chanting used for each portion, from circle casting to dismissal. It was after sunset and the dark pressed in through the windows as we gathered and sang. The altar was decorated for Brigid with a small votive candle in the center lit especially for her.

Before we even reached the point of the ritual where we were going to chant and invoke Brigid, the small candle dedicated to her burned down and went out. Where I was standing I watched the flame die and the curl of dark smoke rise, and then it too went out. We sang another song, and the smoke dissipated, then we were told that the song for Brigid was going to be sung and the main portion of the rite would commence. I remember thinking what a pity it was that her candle hadn't lasted long enough to at least burn while we called her in, but something like five to ten minutes had now passed since it had gone out.

Kellianna started singing. People held hands, and sang the chorus with her. A feeling of warmth and friendship began to fill the room and people started to smile as they sang, many closing their eyes. It was a beautiful moment, and I thought I could really feel Brigid's presence for the first time in my life.

And then I happened to glance down at the altar and saw the Brigid candle flicker back to life, the flame jumping up and then settling into a steady burn. I did a double take, unable to stop myself, and then looked away, only to meet the eyes of a man part way across the circle who caught me looking at him and silently mouthed, 'Did you see that?'

I looked back to be sure it was actually burning and not some trick of the light or mistake before nodding slightly and silently answering, 'Yes.'

My eyes remained fixed on the candle for the rest of the song, and I have to confess I didn't do much singing. I held my breath, expecting it to go out any moment, but it burned steadily as everyone sang. Right up until the end of the song, and then as the last word vibrated in the air and silence filled the small space in that afterglow that can happen sometimes after a particularly good ritual moment, the candle went out again. No fanfare, no drama, the flame simply dropped down and ceased to be.

Before the ritual continued several people mentioned the candle re-lighting and there was nervous laughter and more smiles and general delight. And then the moment passed and the ritual went on. But for me, that moment was a defining one, where I not only knew in my heart that Brigid was there, but I also saw the proof of it with my eyes.

Chapter Two

Brigid by Other Names

Deae Victoriae Brigantiae aram dedit Aurelius Senopianus
Inscription to Brigantia from Yorkshire

To the Goddess Victory Brigantia this altar is given by Aurelius Senopianus
(M. Daimler, 2015)

Brigid is a pan-Celtic Goddess and while the bulk of her mythology today comes to us from Ireland, historically she was found across the different Celtic cultures. In this chapter we will look at Brigid's appearances in those different cultures. Certain common feature will be fairly obvious between the different 'Brig' Goddesses and it is easy to see why scholars view her as a pan-Celtic deity. One might theorize a path for this Goddess based on the available evidence, from Gaul to England to Ireland and then to Scotland and Wales, from pagan Goddess to Catholic saint – and back again to pagan Goddess today.

Brigid in Gaul – Brigandu

The Gaulish Brigandu is nearly identical to the British Brigantia, and both names have identical meanings and linguistic roots. Place names suggest she was found all across Europe at one time (Ross, 1967). She has no surviving mythology or folklore and what we do know about her comes from archeological remains and linguistics, but those sources do still have some value. Brigandu's name is etymologically related to Brigid's and probably comes from the older proto-Indo-European root bhreg meaning 'high'. Another variant of her name on the European continent is 'Briga', which is close to the Old Irish version of her name Brig (O hOgain, 2006). It is likely that Brigandu is the Goddess whom Caesar in his *Gallic Wars* equated to Minerva, saying the Gauls believed, 'Minerva imparts the invention of manufactures' (O hOgain, 2006; MacDevitt, 2009). This particular view of Brigandu seems similar to Brigid of Smithcraft.

Brigid in England – Brigantia

Brigid's cognate in Britain was Brigantia. Brigantia was the special Goddess of the Brigantes who lived in the territory that is now northern England, specifically the Yorkshire area (Ross, 1970). Professor Dáithí O hOgain suggests that it was the immigration of some of the Brigantes tribe to Ireland in the 1st century C.E. that brought the Goddess there, specifically to south-eastern Ireland (O hOgain, 2006). We know that the name Brigantia comes from the root brigantī, meaning high or exalted one. Because England was conquered by Rome fairly early and Roman paganism then influenced native beliefs, which were later further eroded by Christianity and waves of other invading cultures, we have no surviving mythology relating to Brigantia. As with Brigandu, what we know about Brigantia comes from linguistics, archaeology, and also from how the Romans related to her. The Romans had a practice called interpretatio Romana where they looked at the deities in areas they occupied and syncretized those Gods to their own. Through this process Brigantia was syncretized to Victory/Victoria and Minerva in her war aspect. In images of her Brigantia is depicted wearing a crown (Ross, 1967). As Brigantia-Minerva she had a temple in England, which featured a perpetual flame just as her Irish counterpart did (Puhvel, 1987). In inscriptions, Brigantia is associated with water and possibly with healing wells and springs (Ross, 1967). From these clues we can surmise that Brigantia was a powerful deity, one who an entire tribal group was named for, and that she was a Goddess of war and victory in battle, and also of fire and probably of healing.

Brigid in Scotland – Bride

Brigid in Scotland is known as Bride, and is far more strongly intertwined with 'Saint Bride' than the Irish Brigid. Her special day was Imbolc, called there 'Là Fèill Bhrìde', the feast of Bride, and celebrated as it was in Ireland on February 1st. The bulk of mythology in Scotland surrounding Bride on Imbolc places her in opposition with the winter Goddess the Cailleach. In some places Bride is seen as having a brother named Angus, seeming to reflect the Irish mythology, but in other areas Angus is Bride's lover or spouse.

The Scottish Bride was particularly associated with childbirth and was prayed to during labor and delivery. Carmichael preserved a folk ritual wherein the midwife would stand in a doorway, brace her hands on the doorframe and chant:

> Bride! Bride! Come in,
> You're welcome is truly made,
> May you give relief to the woman.
> (Ross, 1976)

Bride, like Brigid, appears to be a mother Goddess with healing aspects, and there are many healing wells in Scotland dedicated to her (Beith, 1995). Besides sharing her Irish counterpart's patronage of healing, poetry, and smithcraft, the Scottish Bride was also connected to marriage and guarding the hearth (McNeill, 1959).

Brigid in Wales – Ffraid

Brigid in Wales is known to us through the stories of saint Ffraid – the Welsh version of Brigid's name – and likely reflects stories carried to Wales by the Irish who settled there around the 7th century. Although only known through the lens of the Catholic saint, Ffraid's stories do appear to have potentially older pagan overtones, including an association with Imbolc and the almost ubiquitous miraculous feeding of the poor for which Brigid was known among the Irish. In Welsh belief, Ffraid was an Irish nun who produced honey from stone, turned ashes to butter, and reeds to fish; when her father presented her with a suitor she didn't want to marry she plucked out her eye and was able to put it back in later (Baring-Gould, & Fisher, 1913).

It is possible that the Welsh word for king, 'brenin', may come from the title Brigantinos meaning 'spouse of the exalted one' (Waddell, 2014). This would present a linguistic tie back to the British and Gaulish Goddess Brigantia/Brigandu. It also might hint at older pagan practices where the king would have ritually married the sovereign Goddess of the land in order to establish his right to rule (Waddell, 2014).

Pagan Goddess, Catholic Saint

[Saint Brigid] is the goddess in a threadbare Christian cloak
Sir James Frazer

Our modern understanding of Brigid is largely the result of a blending of the features of the pagan Goddess and Catholic saint (Clark, 1991). There is a sharp divide among scholars on the subject of how closely tied the two may be, with some like Kim McCone stating that saint Brigid, particularly in her later stories, shows a clear separation from the pagan Brigid, while others like Marie-Louise Sjoestedt say that the saint is an accurate preservation of the Goddess. This makes it difficult and at times almost impossible to untangle one from the other, particularly from material that dates to the transition period when Ireland was still nominally pagan and not yet entirely Christian. We can see this for example in the proliferation of both mythic figures and saints named Brigid as well as the characteristics of the early saint Brigid, which clearly reflected earlier mythic patterns, such as providing food and drink to those in need (McCone, 2000). In the

Lebor Gabala Erenn we are told that the Dagda is Brigid's father and that he also had a son named Aed; interestingly saint Brigid also was associated with a person named Aed, in this case a fellow saint. Saint Aed was said to have founded a monastery with buildings dedicated to saint Brigid and saint Brigid was said to have invoked the name of saint Aed to miraculously cure a headache (McCone, 2000). Those seeking to connect to the Goddess today will have to decide for themselves what they feel genuinely reflects older pagan beliefs and what may have evolved in the later Christian period.

We have two main sources for information on saint Brigid: the 7th century *Vita Brigitae*, written in Latin, and the Irish *Bethu Brigte*, both translating to 'Life of Brigid' from their respective languages. They include many fantastic details of the saint's early life, including a strange fire that was said to occur when she was only a child – it engulfed the house she was in, but did not consume it (Green, 1995). It is said she was the child of a Druid and that her mother was a slave, that she was born in a doorway at sunrise, and that she was fed from the milk of an Otherworldly white cow. All of these are very liminal features, which place Brigid between two things, and also reflect older pagan cosmology. Such details may be the attempts of the monks recording her life to make her seem extremely holy, or it is possible they reflect the euhemerization of a Goddess into a human figure that would be acceptable to the new religion. One example of this combining of the pagan myth with Christian saint may be seen in the story of saint Brigid responding to someone who challenged her sanctity by picking up a lit coal from a fire and carrying it a great distance; when she finally dropped it a healing well sprung up where the still burning coal struck the earth (MacNeill, 1962; Patterson, 1994). In this story we may perhaps see traces of Brigid as a Goddess of the forge and of healing, although it is impossible to be certain. It is worth considering that there is no evidence that saint Brigid ever existed as a historic person and that her life appears to be entirely legend (Green, 1995).

Saint Brigid is most strongly associated with Kildare where her church stands near her sacred healing well; the church itself features a perpetual flame tended by Brigadine nuns. Although the perpetual flame cannot be traced with certainty back to the Irish pagan period, Brigid's British counterpart Brigantia had a temple under the guise of Brigantia-Minerva, which also featured a perpetual flame (Puhvel, 1987). Saint Brigid's fire at Kildare was tended only by women, and it was said by one 12th century commentator that despite the great amounts of wood used, no ashes ever collected where the fire burned (O Duinn, 2002). This fire, which has been revived in modern times, was tended by nuns for 19 straight days, but on the 20th it was left to saint Brigid's keeping.

The Irish saint Brigid and the Scottish saint Bride are believed to be both the midwife and foster-mother of Jesus Christ and both are very strongly associated with childbirth, potentially reflecting older mother Goddess concepts. Much like Brigid Brigiu, saint Brigid was strongly associated with caring for those in need and guests (O Duinn, 2002). Also, just as the Goddess was associated with two great oxen, the saint was profoundly tied to cows, so much so that one of her epithets in Scotland was 'Bride of the Kine'[7] (Green, 1995).

Saint Brigid also has a rather fascinating association with love magic. In a tale, which appears in various versions from the 8th through 12th centuries in Ireland, we see a man going to Saint Brigid and requesting an 'epaid'[8] (a spoken spell or physical charm) that will make his wife love him (Borsje, 2012). The saint provides what he has requested, either by having him sprinkle his wife with blessed water or by having him sain the house and bed with it when the she is away, with the desired effect (Borsje, 2012). It is interesting to note that such actions and use of magic were clearly illegal in the law tracts, but in this case is included in the story of the life of a saint. The result of this holy love magic for the man is a wife who loves him so much she cannot bear being parted from his side (Borsje, 2012).

All of the various Brigid-associated saints are honored on the pagan holiday of Imbolc, but Brigid is also honored on Candlemas, which occurs the next day, February 2nd. While Imbolc was a holiday with almost certain pagan roots tied to the Goddess, and possibly reflecting wider Indo-European mother festivals, Candlemas was decidedly Christian in tone and focused on the purification of the Virgin Mary after Christ's birth (Patterson, 1994). There is some debated etymology that suggests that the word Imbolc might itself be related to the verb folcaim, meaning 'I wash' and relate to the idea of ritual purification, but this is uncertain (Patterson, 1994). If true though it might tie the two holidays more closely together and hint at a deeper purification symbolism to Imbolc itself. There is a reference in the 16th century *Hibernica Minora* to Imbolc practices that involved tasting food stores and washing the head, hands and feet (Meyer, 1894). The food tasting is probably a simple way to be certain that winter food stores are still edible and it is likely that the washing represents a genuine medieval Imbolc practice that was lost in later Irish folk practices.

Another rather odd story that is usually attributed to saint Patrick, but is also found with saint Brigid as the heroic protagonist, seeks to explain why people give a blessing to those who sneeze (MacNeill, 1962). The story goes that there was a monster named Suicín who produced a terrible light at night that would cause fatal sneezing fits in anyone who saw it. One night the saint was passing through the area and upon seeking shelter for the night found out about the monster and so set about to defeat it. Various methods are given in different versions of the story including making the sign of the cross or producing a candle that created a counter-light, and in one version the saint teaches the people to give a blessing after a person sneezes to break the evil spell (MacNeill, 1962). In this way the monster is defeated and right order restored, and the idea of blessing those who sneeze to protect them begins.

Brigid in My Life

When I first became pagan in the early 1990s I had no resources except a handful of popular pagan books. This wasn't a bad thing of course and it's the way that many people got started and still get started; it wasn't until a few years later that my focus became more Reconstructionist and I started looking at the source material itself. So in those early years I celebrated Imbolc on February 2nd and with a decidedly Candlemas-like approach. My understanding of Brigid then was rudimentary, a child's under-standing (I was 11 when I first started reading about paganism), but I liked envisioning her as a tall beautiful lady with flame red hair and a gentle smile.

When I decided that it was essential for me to do a self-dedication to the pagan path, just like all my books talked about, I chose Imbolc to do it on. At that point the holiday to me was on the 2nd, the same day America celebrates Groundhog's Day, and was about cleansing and blessing of the self, so it seemed ideal for a self-dedication. I got everything together and when the night of the ritual arrived I was excited to take such a life changing step. At 13, coming from a non-religious background, doing something like this was momentous and I felt like I was ready to commit myself to the spirituality I had been studying.

I went out alone into the bitter cold, without a winter coat on, and tried to do my ritual the way I had learned to, but it was hard to focus. February in Connecticut is frigid and the darkness on that particular night was total, without any moon to light my way. It was Brigid's holiday, so I automatically started calling on her, asking for her help, for the strength to get through what I planned to do. At the time it was almost a reflex to call on a Goddess I associated with warmth and light under those circumstances. It was important to me to make a declaration of my religious path, the books I'd read at that point had emphasized the need to be outdoors, and I was too stubborn to let the cold weather stop me. So I prayed to Brigid.

It's funny the way, as children, we simply take experiences in our stride, without considering them at all out of the ordinary. I don't remember ever feeling Brigid's presence or having a sense of the numinous, but I prayed and then I was warm. The cold simply ceased to be something I noticed, as if everything around me had become an indoor room temperature. I took the usual half hour or so kneeling on the cold ground to do my ritual, dedicating myself to the Irish Gods and to pagan spirituality. And then I got up, collected my supplies and went back inside, feeling euphoric.

At the time it never even registered that what I did was dangerous or that I was risking frostbite and hypothermia. And I never stopped and thought that it should seem at all remarkable to pray to Brigid for warmth and then be warm. It all seemed entirely natural and normal.

We speak, and the Gods really do listen. Sometimes they even answer.

Chapter Three

Brigid in Mythology

Trí labra ata ferr táu: ochán ríg do chath, sreth immais, molad iar lúag.
Triads of Ireland

Three speeches better than silence: inciting a king to battle, using alliteration, praise after payment.[9]
(M. Daimler)

Unfortunately the older Gaulish and British myths have not survived so when it comes to sources for Brigid's myths we must look primarily to the Irish and Scottish material, particularly for the pagan texts. Luckily we do have a large amount of this material to draw on and it can tell us a lot about the Goddess. The Irish texts are older, generally, and more likely to reflect the pagan beliefs prior to Christian influence, although we can't be entirely sure to what degree. The Scottish material was written down later and seems to show a blend of influences from the native culture and the Dal Riada Irish who settled portions of Western Scotland in the 6th and 7th centuries.

The Irish Sources

The Cath Maige Tuired
The *Cath Maige Tuired* is a 16th century text believed to date back to between the 9th and 12th centuries, which tells the story of a war between the chthonic Fomorians and the divine Tuatha Dé Danann. The Tuatha Dé Danann had previously won a battle against the Fir Bolg, a primal race of beings who had control of Ireland when the Gods arrived, but in the process the high king

Nuada lost his arm. The Tuatha Dé Danann had a law that no king could rule who was not whole and so Nuada stepped down and the Gods chose as his successor the half-Fomorian, half-Dé Danann warrior Eochaid Bres. Bres's mother was the sovereignty Goddess Eriu, one of the Tuatha Dé Danann, and his father was Elatha, a king of the Fomorians. Unfortunately Bres proved to be an unworthy king and allowed his father's people to put a heavy tax on the Tuatha Dé Danann, which eventually caused them to rebel and oust him as king, starting a war. As the war was about to commence, we are told that Bres and Brigid (here named Bric) had a son together, Ruadán, and this son chose to act on the side of his father's people by infiltrating the Tuatha Dé Danann and trying to kill the divine smith Goibniu. Instead Ruadán was himself killed by the smith, and we are told:

Tic Brich ocus caines a mac. Éghis artós, goilis fodeod. Conud andsin roclos gol ocus egem artos a n-Erinn. Is si didiu an Prich sin roairich feit do caismert a n-oidci. (Gray, 1983)

Brigid came and keened her son. Screamed loudly, wept finally. This was the first time that weeping and loud screaming were heard in Ireland. And she was thus the Brigid that had devised a whistling to signal by night. (Translation, M. Daimler 2015)

The appearance of Brigid in the story is brief, but profound. We learn that she had a child with the high king Bres, who we assume was her husband, and that her son was killed prompting her to be the first person ever to caoin (keen) in Ireland, a type of ritualized wailing in grief that was outlawed as a pagan practice by the later Christian church. The establishment of this type of grieving by Brigid is significant because of the idea that an action by a human has importance as a re-enactment of something originally done by a deity which is considered ubiquitous in ancient cultures (O Cathasaigh, 2014). We keen in grief because we are following the lead of the Goddess who established the practice as the proper way to show grief. We also learn from this passage that Brigid created a whistle or type of whistling noise that was used as a signal at night, possibly during times of conflict.

Lebor Gabala Erenn

The *Lebor Gabala Erenn*, or the *Book of the Taking of Ireland*, is the story of the different waves of invasions that occurred as five groups of divine or semi-divine peoples settled Ireland and then fought with newcomers over the island, ending with the arrivals of the Gaels. The book exists in multiple versions found in different manuscripts and dates to around the 11th century. It tells the story of Ireland in the form of a pseudo-history with real events and cultures liberally intermixed with both pagan and Christian mythology. Brigid appears in the fourth volume of the book, which tells the story of the Tuatha Dé Danann and their fight against first the Fir Bolg and then the Fomorians:

Brigit banfile ingen in Dagda is oce ro baí Fe ocus Mean, dá rígh-damraidi, diatá Femen. Is oce ro baí Triath rí a torcraide, diatá Treithirne. Is oce ro baí ro clossa trí gotha diabul íar n-imarbus in Erinn, .i. Fet ocus Go locus Eigem.

Ocus os lei ro baí Cirb rí moltraigi, diatá Mag cirb. Is leo ro boí Cerman ocus Cermat ocus In Mac Oc. (Macalister, 1940)

Brigit the poetess, daughter of the Dagda, with her were Fe and Men, the two kings of oxen, from whom is Femen [called]. And with her was Triath, king of her boars, from whom is Treithirne [called]. And with her were heard, the three demonic sounds after transgressions[10] in Ireland, whistling and weeping and lamentation.[11]

And also with her was Cirb king of the rams, from whom is Mag Cirb [called]. With them were Cerman and Cermat and the Mac Oc. (Translation Daimler, 2015)

This brief passage in the *Lebor Gabala Erenn* is nonetheless very illuminating. From it we are not only reminded that Brigid is a poetess, but also that she possessed four significant animals, all of which are kings of their respective species. The two oxen gave their names to the plain of Barrow in County Carlow, and Magh Feimhin in County Tipperary; and likewise another plain in Tipperary was named for her boar (O hOgain, 2006). We do not know what plain was named after her ram, Cirb, but he, like the others, is said to be the king of all rams, and one may assume therefore all sheep. It may also be worth noting the meanings of the names of the animals: Fe – lamentation; Men – a mouth, possibly also dust; Triath – a king, noble, boar, hill; Cirb – sharp, cutting.

The listing of her animals is followed by a listing of three male Tuatha Dé Danann described as being 'with them', two of whom we know are Brigid's half-brothers Cermait and Óengus, here simply called by his epithet of 'Mac Oc' or young son. It is tempting to assume the third name also belongs to one of her brothers, but Cerman is an obscure name. One early 20th century text suggests that he was the local God of Ulster roughly analogous to Crom Cruach elsewhere, but provides no sources for the idea (Mahon, 1919).

Other Sources

Sanas Cormac
The *Sanas Cormac*, or *Cormac's Glossary*, is a collection of the meanings of words and etymologies, often quite fanciful. The text exists today in pieces found in a variety of other manuscripts and is believed to date back to the early 1400s. Although the meanings given to the words are often clearly inventions of the time, they nonetheless can provide some profound insight into how the people understood these concepts and in this case what the beliefs about Brigid as a pagan Goddess were at that point.

Brigit .i. banfile ingen in Dagdai. is eiside Brigit baneceas (ł be neicsi) .i. Brigit bandee noadradís filid. arba romor 7 baroán afri thgnam. is airesin ideo eam (deam) uocant poetarum hoc nomine cuius sorores erant Brigit bé legis Brigit bé goibnechta .i. bandé .i. tri hingena in Dagdai insin. de quarum nominibus pene omnes Hibernenses dea Brigit uocabatur. Brigit din .i. breoaigit ł breoṡaigit. (Sanas Cormac, n.d.)

Brigit – a poet, daughter of the Dagda. This Brigit is a woman of poetry (female poet) that is Brigit the Goddess worshipped by poets because her protection was very great and well known. This is why she is called a Goddess by poets. Her sisters were Brigit the woman of healing and Brigit the woman of smithcraft, Goddesses; they are three daughters of the Dagda. Almost all Irish Goddesses are called a Brigit. Brigit then from breoaigit or breoshaigit, [fiery arrow].
(Translation, M. Daimler, 2015)

This is probably one of the key passages about Brigid from a modern pagan perspective as it is from this in particular that we get the idea of Brigid as Goddess of healing and smithcraft. Brigid as a poet and Goddess of poets is a common idea found in multiple sources (Gray, 1983). However, her connection to smiths and healing is only found explicitly stated here. We also learn here that all the Brigids were daughters of the Dagda, and that Brigid's renown was so great that, as the glossary puts it 'almost all Irish Goddesses are called a Brigit'. Although it is unlikely that all Goddesses actually were called Brigid this may be further proof both of her significance and of her name as an epithet in itself meaning high or exalted. The glossary then goes on to suggest an entirely fanciful etymology of 'fiery arrow' as the source of her name; although we know now that isn't the etymology of Brigid, it gives us the added information that she was associated with fire and with arrows, which may relate to smithcraft or possibly hint at a martial aspect.

Imcallam in da Thurad
In this text, two poets – one older, one a youth – get into a battle of words over who is the superior. At one point the youth is asked whose son he is and in his reply he lists the three Gods of Danu. A gloss on this section of text in the *Lebar na Núachongbála* clarifies:

> The three gods of Dana the three sons of Brigit the poetess, that is Brian, Luchar, and Uar, the three sons of Bres, son of Eladan, and Brigit the poetess, daughter of the great Dagda, king of Ireland, was their mother; and one of his [Dagda's] names was Ruad Rofessa; and Cermait, Dermait, and Aed [were the names of his sons]. (Guyonvarc'h, 1999)

This gloss reinforces Brigit's connections to different people, including Bres and that the three Gods of Dana[12] – which can be translated as Gods of skill or Gods of art – are her sons. It also reminds us that the Dagda is her father and lists Cermait and Aed as her brothers as well as the obscure Dermait. More than all this though the passage in *Imcallam in da Thurad* shows that Brigid was so significant as a Goddess of poets that a poet trying to prove himself might trace his lineage, at least figuratively, back to Brigid.

Lebar na Núachongbála: 'Slan Seiss'
The Book of Leinster also includes this 9th century poem to Brigid that reinforces the idea that she is a Goddess of sovereignty:

> Slán seiss, a Brigit co mbúaid, for grúaid Lifi lir co tráig; is tú banfhlaith buidnib slúaig fil for clannaib Cathaír Máir.
> ...
> A Brigit 'sa tír ad-chíu, is cách a úair immud—rá, ro gab do chlú for a chlú ind ríg, is tú forda-tá.
> ...
> Táthut bithfhlaith lasin Ríg cen a tír i fil do rúaim; a ué Bresail maic Déin, slán seiss, a Brigit co mbúaid.

Sit thou safely enthroned, triumphant Brigit, upon the side of Liffey far as the strand of the ebbing sea!

Thou art the sovereign lady with banded hosts that presides over the Children of Catháir the Great.

[A list is given of different Irish kings and their fate.]

Brigit is the smile that smiles on you from the plain...of Core's land; of each generation which it reared in turn Liffey of Lore has made ashes.

[The list of kings continues.]

Oh Brigit whose land I behold, on which each one in turn has moved about, thy fame has outshone the fame of the king — thou art over them all.

Thou hast everlasting rule with the king apart from the land wherein is thy cemetery. Grand-child of Bresal son of Dian, sit thou safely enthroned, triumphant Brigit! (Meyer, 1912)

It is likely that this poem was meant to be for the saint; however, there are strong pagan deity overtones such as the opening line calling Brigid 'banfhlaith', sovereign lady or woman of sovereignty and then listing the names and deeds of a variety of kings of Ireland. The poem also refers to the land of Ireland as her land and says that her fame is greater than the king's.

The Lake of Beer

A late first millennia poem attributed to saint Brigid strongly relates the saint to brewing. Several beer-related miracles were said to have been performed by Brigid, including transforming bathwater to beer and providing enough beer for all her churches for a week from just a handful of malt. Although these are clearly attributed to the Catholic saint, they do resonate with pagan concepts, and could possibly reflect older beliefs that may have once been attributes of Brigid as a Goddess of smithcraft, although this is only supposition. The poem is as follows:

I'd like to give
a lake of beer to God.
I'd love the Heavenly Host
to be tippling for all eternity.
I'd love the people of Heaven
to live with me.
To dance and sing,
If they wanted,
I'd give for their use
vats of suffering.
I'd make Heaven cheerful
because the happy heart is true,
I'd make the people contented,
I'd like Jesus to be there too.
I'd like the people of Heaven
to gather from all around,
I'd give a special welcome to women,
the three Marys of great renown.
I'd sit with the men and women of God.
There by the lake of beer.
We'd drink good health forever,
and every drop would be prayer.

Scottish Material

Brigid in Scotland, under the guise of Bride, bears many similarities to her Irish counterpart. We find her mostly in the folklore of the people preserved within the past several hundred years by anthropologists and ethnographers. In the 1917 book *Wonder Tales from Scottish Myth and Legend* we learn that Bride was considered to rule over the summer half of the year, from Beltane to Samhain, and that she was considered the fairest Goddess of all (McIntyre, 2015). The other half of the year was under the rule of the Cailleach[13] and there are a variety of stories about how the year changed rulers. In one version Angus is the Cailleach's son and has fallen in love with Bride, so the Cailleach imprisons the other Goddess, causing winter to come to the land; only when Angus finally succeeds in freeing her on Imbolc does winter begin to give up her hold on the land (McIntyre, 2015). According to the story, while she was a captive Bride is given the difficult task of washing a brown wool until it is white, which can only be accomplished with the help of Father Winter; when the Cailleach sees it she is furious and realizes her time has almost passed (MacKenzie, 1917). Her son Angus has been dreaming of Bride and is told by the king of the Land of the Ever Young that when Angus is king of summer, Bride will be his queen so he sets out to find her, eventually succeeding (MacKenzie, 1917). In other versions of the story the Cailleach must drink from a magical spring, either on Imbolc at which point she transforms into Bride, or at Beltane at which point Bride is freed (McNeill; 1959; McIntyre, 2015). The *Carmina Gadelica*, a collection of chants and songs from Scotland at the end of the 19th century, has a variety of chants to Bride relating to Imbolc:

Thig an nathair as an toll
Là donn Brìde,
Ged robh trì troighean dhen t-sneachd
Air leac an làir.

The serpent will come from the hole
On the brown Day of Bríde,
Though there should be three feet of snow
On the flat surface of the ground.
(Carmichael, 1900)

Moch maduinn Bhride,
Thig an nimhir as an toll,
Cha bhoin mise ris an nimhir,
Cha bhoin an nimhir rium.

Early on Bride's morn
The serpent shall come from the hole,
I will not molest the serpent,
Nor will the serpent molest me.
(Carmichael, 1900)

In both of these examples the central idea is that Imbolc is when the adder awakens form its hibernation and emerges, and there are a series of prayers that focus on protection against the snakes.

An 8th century poem credited to saint Bride called Aengus Cèile Dè says:

I should like a great lake of ale
For the king of kings;
I should like the family of heaven
To be drinking it through time eternal.
(Beith, 1995)

Although not referencing Bride herself, this sentiment is attributed to her tying the Scottish Bride, like her Welsh and Irish counterparts, to ale. This concept then would appear to be a pan-Celtic one, where Brigid is associated with the production and consumption of ale or beer.

Welsh Material

The majority of the Welsh material we have about Brigid, or more properly saint Ffraid, is very limited. We have the story of the life of the saint and we also have brief references to her in poetry. An example of this would be:

Digwyl San Ffraid ydeodd fenaid,
I bydd parod pawb ai wyrod

Saint Brigid's day it was, my soul,
Everyone was ready with his drink
(Baring-Gould & Fisher, 1913)

Manx Material

As with the Welsh the Manx material is very limited and places Brigid in the role of an Irish saint who traveled to the Isle of Man where she is called Brede or Breeshey. Her holiday is still celebrated on February 1st, known as Laa'l Breeshey or Brigid's Feast Day (Moore, 1891). The customs surrounding Laa'l Breeshey are identical to the Irish and Scottish, focusing on the visitation of Breeshey to homes overnight, where she is welcomed in, and the search for omens the following morning. Her welcome is made in Manx by saying:

Brede, Brede, tar gys my thie, tar dys thie ayms noght.
Foshil jee yn dorrys da Brede, as lhig da Brede cheet stiagh.

Bridget, Bridget, come to my house, come to my house to-night,
Open the door to Bridget, and let Bridget come in.
(Moore, 1891)

As with the other cultures, rushes and straws are used to make a bed for the Goddess/saint and the fireplace ashes are checked for the mark of her 'club' the next day as a sign of blessing (Moore, 1891).

Brigid in My Life

My first encounter with Brigid in a story didn't come in myth but in modern fiction, which as it happens was how I came across all the Irish Gods before I knew they were Gods or that there were Gods of any sort to be found. When I was young I read a book called *The Hounds of the Morrigan*, which tells the story of a modern brother and sister named Pidge and Brigit who quite accidently come into possession of a book that holds the key to freeing a great evil. In the story the children are guided by the Dagda, as well as several mythic figures like the druid Cathbad and hero Cu Chulainn, to overcome the challenges they face. Two of the forces of good who aid them are named 'Boodie' and 'Patsy' who appear to be threadbare wanderers, but in the end are revealed to be Brigid and her brother Óengus in disguise. The book is amazingly well written, deftly weaving ancient myth and modern fantasy together and I found it utterly captivating as a child.

What appealed to me about Brigid in the novel, indeed what still does appeal to me as Pat O'Shea did a marvelous job of capturing her spirit even in his fiction, was the way that she was simultaneously gentle and fierce, wise and humorous. In the story Brigid is not a one-dimensional character, even though she has only a small part to play, she is deep and complex. Although since then I have come to be very familiar with the variety of mythology around Brigid I still really enjoy re-reading this book.

Chapter Four

Symbols, Animals, and Holidays

On the Feast Day of beautiful Bride,
The flocks are counted on the moor,
The raven goes to prepare the nest,
And again goes the rook.
Traditional Scottish (Carmichael, 1900)

Brigid was the patron Goddess of Leinster in Ireland historically, and her worship has spread far afield from there (Clark, 1991). Kildare in Leinster is strongly associated with Brigid, through the saint who was said to have founded a church there; the name Cill Dara means 'oak church' or 'church of the oak' and from this some people associate the oak with Brigid. In *The Triads of Ireland*, Kildare is called 'cride Hérenn' the heart of Ireland (Meyer, 1906). Echoing earlier stories of Goddesses claiming territory using an item of their clothing to mark out the space, it is said the boundary of Kildare was demarcated by saint Brigid laying out her cloak (Green, 1995). There are a variety of towns in Wales named after Brigid, which can be seen by their inclusion of 'ffraid' within the name. The root of her name, Brigh or Brí, meaning high, is often used in place names for hills and other high places in both Ireland and on the continent, but interestingly her name and other variants of Briga and Briginti are also commonly used in river names in Wales, England, and Europe and to a lesser degree in Ireland (O hOgain, 2006). Through this then she is connected to both heights and rivers, two places sacred in Irish cosmology.

Brigid has a special healing well and site at Kildare and is associated with water that has healing powers. In Scotland the MacKenzies are said to possess a healing stone associated with the holy well of Brigid, which would be dipped into the water from the well for a healing charm (McNeill, 1956). In addition there are multiple other healing wells and sacred wells dedicated to Brigid in Ireland and across Scotland.

Brigid also has a special talisman called a brat Bhride (Brigid's mantle or cloak), which is a small piece of cloth left out on Imbolc eve to be blessed by the Goddess/saint, which would then have healing properties throughout the year. By tradition a white cloth is preferred and ideally one of silk (O Duinn, 2002). In some views the brat Bhride becomes more powerful each year that it is used, while in others it must be destroyed after the seventh year and replaced with a new one. This particular item not only had healing powers, but also had protective qualities and was used to guard women delivering babies as well as newborns from being taken by the Fair Folk (O Suilleabhain, 1967).

Brigid's crosses were another important symbol of Brigid, although scholars debate whether they are pagan in origin. The term Brigid's cross is something of a misnomer, however, as they do not all appear with the four-armed shape, some having only three arms and others a more lozenge-like appearance. The crosses are believed to be solar symbols (Green, 1995). In Catholic myth the story goes that saint Brigid was trying to show a cross to someone to convert them and having nothing else at hand wove one from rushes. In other versions of the story the cross was invented to memorialize Brigid making the sign of the cross to save herself from poison, or else to commemorate a miracle where she used the sign of the cross to produce an abundant supply of cheese (O Duinn, 2002). However, there is evidence of similar symbols dating back much further than the common era being found on what are presumed to be Goddess figures; in these cases the symbol is believed to represent fertility (O Duinn, 2002). The Brigid's cross was made new at each Imbolc, and the old ones kept, so that over time some houses would amass a large collection of them. They were believed to be effective protection against illness in the home, as well as drawing fertility and luck; in southern Ireland they were used like the brat Bhride, being placed directly upon an ill person's body in order to impart healing energy (O Duinn, 2002).

Brigid possessed the two kings of the oxen as well as the king of boars and king of rams. Here as in so many other things we see Brigid's appeal to people across society being demonstrated in the animals associated with her, because each of the three types of animals whose kings belonged to her were related to a different group within society. Cattle were the sign of kings and nobility, pigs the mark of the common man and lordless warriors, and sheep were the dominion of women (Patterson, 1994). Brigid then is ultimately the Goddess of all of these types of livestock, and by extension of each societal class associated with them.

It is impossible to overemphasize the importance of cows in early Irish culture. Cattle were the currency of the day, the thing which people fought wars over, and the mark of a king's status. Although horses were more prestigious to own, the cow was a sign of wealth and oxen allowed for greater cultivation of land; so important were cows that terms like 'calf' and 'young heifer' were used in the same way an English speaker might use 'darling' (Patterson, 1994). Cattle are frequent motifs in artwork because of the herding culture found among the Celts and they represent prosperity and abundance (Green, 1992). It has even been suggested that the design of the ring forts, which are ubiquitous across Ireland, were originally meant to protect cattle from being stolen during raids, reflecting their profound social importance (McCormick, 2008). For Brigid to possess not one but two oxen described as kings is significant as oxen were used for ploughing, and were thought to be the ideal animals for that purpose. Through her oxen Brigid is associated with cultivation and the abundance of the earth.

Pigs were the most common livestock animal eaten in Ireland, as they reproduced quickly and ate a variety of foods that could be easily found in forests (Patterson, 1994). Pigs were also often associated with feasting, with pig bones being the most common faunal remains found at Emhain Macha and the second most common at Teamhair and Dun Ailinne (McCormick, 2010). Interestingly pigs were also associated with the fían, the warrior bands, for whom wild boar meat was often viewed as the ubiquitous food (Patterson, 1994). This may indicate another connection between Brigid and warriors. Pigs were an easy animal to keep and required less tending due to their high intelligence, but could be destructive as they are prone to eating anything and do not distinguish between planted crops and fallen masts.

Sheep in Irish culture were uniquely the province of women, and while they provided several different resources for the household they conveyed no special status (Patterson, 1994). As anyone who has ever handled sheep before knows, they can be difficult animals and are thoroughly creatures of habit. This difficulty in dealing with them and the stubbornness with which they would cling to familiar places may have been one reason why they never held a high social status in Ireland and why they become the purview of women (Patterson, 1994). The value of sheep lay mainly in the production of wool and of milk, both of which were also thoroughly in the domain of women and this may also have contributed to the association. Brigid's possession of the king of rams, and one assumes therefore all sheep, solidifies her connection to sheep and to sheep's milk, which is more clearly shown in the strong dairy associations of her holiday Imbolc. On Imbolc it is not cows' milk that is celebrated but sheep's milk and the fresh nutrition it represented.

According to Carmichael, Brigid's special bird in Scotland is the oystercatcher, which in Scottish Gaidhlig is named Bridein, 'Bride's bird', and Gille Bride, 'servant of Bride' (Carmichael, 1900). The linnet is also special to the Goddess and is named bigein Bride, 'little bird of Bride'; it is said to whistle its song to her each morning (McNeill, 1959). In Scottish myth it is said that the linnet was the first bird to greet Bride after Angus freed her from the Cailleach on Imbolc, earning its name this way, and the oystercatcher was the first bird on the seashore to greet her and was then given its name (Mackenzie, 1917). Saint Brigid's sacred bird in Ireland was the skylark and to hear the lark sing on Imbolc morning would bring good luck for the entire year (Anderson, 2008). In Wales a particular fish that featured in a miracle performed by Ffraid, the smelt, is called the Pysgod Sant Ffraid in Welsh, meaning 'fish of saint Brigid' (Baring-Gould, & Fisher, 1913).

Brigid's flower in Scotland is the dandelion, called beàrnan Brìghde, the 'notched plant of Bride' (Beithe, 1995). Dandelion has several medicinal and folk uses, and is a very useful plant as well as being pleasing to look at. It is used as a cure for stomach problems and ulcers and the root can be dried and ground to make a coffee-like drink (Beith, 1995). In Scottish tradition, the dandelion's 'milk' is said to feed lambs (McNeill, 1959).

Imbolc – Brigid's holiday

Imbolc is a holy day dedicated to the Goddess Brigid and celebrated on February 1st, although Carmichael mentions an older date as well of February 13th.[14] The *Carmina Gadelica* mentions several traditions relating to this holiday, a holiday specially dedicated to Brigid in both Ireland and Scotland. Although Imbolc as it's celebrated today is blend of folk traditions dedicated to saint Brigid, it was undoubtedly originally a pagan holiday celebrating the very beginning of the agricultural year (O Duinn, 2002). It was right around the time of Imbolc each year that the sheep would begin lambing, and indeed the oldest explanation for the meaning of the holiday's name, although likely inaccurate, relates to this. In the Tochmarc Emire, which gives both the name Imbolc and the alternate Oimelc,[15] we are told:

To Oimolc, i.e., the beginning of spring, viz., different (ime) is its
wet (folc), viz the wet of spring, and the wet of winter. Or, oi-melc,
viz., oi, in the language of poetry, is a name for sheep, whence oibá
sheep's death is named, as bath is a name for 'death'. Oi-melc, then,
is the time in which the sheep come out and are milked, whence oisc
(a ewe), i.e., oisc viz., barren sheep. (Meyer, 1890)

Of the four Irish fire festivals, Imbolc is the most family oriented, although it does also have wider community aspects. In ancient Ireland marriages were often contracted and made during the winter, consummated in spring, and children were born in the period leading up to Imbolc, tying the birth of new children into the time when the new lambs were being born (Patterson, 1994). While we don't have any surviving information about the ancient ways that this day was celebrated we do have a plethora of native traditions to draw on, with the role of saint Brigit and the pagan Goddess Brigid often blurred and easily shifted fully into paganism. With some slight alteration, all of these traditions can be celebrated by any pagan or pagan family to honor Imbolc and the holiday's main deity, Brigid.

A basic overview of the Irish traditions, most of which were actively practiced into the last century, is helpful in giving the reader both an understanding of the holiday and of ways that it can be adapted for modern practice. There were often regional variations in practice and even in the tone of the celebrations, from solemn to comical, which created a wide array of different traditions associated with this holiday (Danaher, 1972). For the purposes of modern celebration by a pagan household it would be best to focus on specific traditions and choose one tone for the festival, rather than trying to include everything noted here.

Generally it was the daughters of the household who played the main roles, although the mother might also be called to do so if there were no daughters. This is in contrast to other holidays, which place the father as the main actor in any rituals, divination, or prayers, and establish the more domestic tone of Imbolc. The prominence of women and daughters also demonstrates the importance placed on Brigid at this holiday, with the women and girls often being the main intercessors between Brigid and the family in the ritual enacted or playing the role of Brigid herself. Imbolc also places a strong emphasis on children's participation that is lacking at other holidays, which tend to have a more adult tone.

Weaving new Brigid's crosses – symbols of protection, health, and blessing – was an important Imbolc tradition in many places. One ritual that was enacted in Connaught, Sligo, Leitrim, Mayo, Roscommon, and Ulster before the Brigid's crosses were woven for the new year on the eve of the festival was for the eldest daughter to take the part of Brigid and wait outside carrying the material for the project (Danaher, 1972). She would then knock three times, proclaiming herself to be Brigid requesting entrance; she would then be warmly welcomed in and the family would sit down to dinner with an elaborate blessing prayer (Danaher, 1972). The meal often prominently featured dairy products, and if the family was wealthy might also include fresh mutton (Danaher, 1972). After eating the meal the family would sit and weave the new crosses, with the largest sprinkled with water and hung up on the wall until the next Imbolc (Danaher, 1972). In parts of Leitrim there was also a children's practice to use a small rectangle of wood and with potato paste attach peeled rushes in shapes symbolizing the moon, sun, and stars, which would be hung up alongside the woven crosses (Danaher, 1972). Interestingly, although weaving the Brigid's crosses was traditional, other activities that involved twisting or turning motions such as ploughing, spinning or digging were prohibited by custom (O Suilleabhain, 1967).

Another tradition was to create an effigy or doll, called a brideog (little Brigid), representing Brigid. The Brideog might be made of straw from the last sheaf of the harvest, leftover rushes from weaving the crosses, a repurposed child's doll, or the dash from the butter churn. The effigy would be decorated with a white dress and mask or carved turnip, and might be comical, grotesque, or beautiful in appearance (Danaher, 1972). In some parts of Ireland the Brideog was carefully and elaborately decorated with shells, crystals, and other natural adornments (Carmichael, 1900). In some places, including Ulster, Connaught, Leinster and Munster, the children would process from house to house carrying the brideog and pronouncing Brigid's blessing on each home (Danaher, 1972). At each home the people would give gifts to the effigy, and the mother of the household would give food to the children in the procession, usually cheese, butter, or bread; this food would later be used by the children for a feast of their own (Carmichael, 1900). In other areas including Cork, Clare, Galway, Mayo, and Kildare, a brideog might not be used, but rather the unmarried girls would form the procession with one of their number chosen to represent Brigid (Danaher, 1972). In Ulster it was said that the chosen girl wore a crown of rushes, called a crothán Brighite, and carried a shield (sgaith Bhrighite) on her arm; she carried Brigid's crosses to hand out telling each household that it was the sword of Brigid (Danaher, 1972). Although attributed to the saint one might imagine a connection to the pagan Goddess, and possibly to her obscure war aspect in these particular actions. In other areas the procession might collect food from each house, and in some cases might be comprised entirely of men or boys who would play music at each house (Danaher, 1972). In these cases the procession was often referred to as 'Biddy Boys' (EstynEvans, 1957).

In those homes that used an effigy as a Brideog, a small bed would be prepared, made of rushes or of birch twigs, on the eve of Imbolc (Estyn Evans, 1957). In some cases the older women in the home would prepare or shape a small cradle, the leaba Bride or bed of Brigid, for the effigy to sleep in (Carmichael, 1900). In this tradition the effigy was made with great care and a ritual enacted, much like the one mentioned earlier with the reeds for the crosses, where the effigy was taken outside and invited in. In one tradition the women of the house prepared everything and then one stood in the open door, bracing on the door jambs, and loudly invited Brigid in three times, telling her that her bed is ready (Carmichael, 1900). The brideog was placed in the bed with a small wand, the slat Brighid, which may be made of birch, hazel, willow or another white wood (Carmichael, 1900). In some places the night would end with a piece of bread or handful of oats being thrown against the doorstep to symbolically banish hunger for the coming year (O Suilleabhain, 1967). The brat Bhride and Brid's crosses were often placed outside and a welcoming fire left burning all night with the belief that Brigid herself would pass by and bless the home; this seems to reflect an older pagan belief as it is atypical of a Catholic saint's day celebration (O Duinn, 2002). Although not generally found in Catholic belief, the idea of a deity or fairy being visiting a specific place at a specific time is found in other Irish myths and practices, such as those around Áine Chliach[16] (O Duinn, 2002).

The practices follow a basic pattern, where a large meal is prepared on the night before the date of the holiday, a ceremony is acted out where Brigid is invited in, the meal is eaten, a symbol of Brigid is made and placed in the home overnight or else the Brideog is put to bed by the hearth, and divination is taken, usually the next morning. Within this basic outline the variations occur at different points depending on the location's traditions. Generally the traditions of the northern counties emphasized children and girls more, while the south had Biddy Boys; both included family celebrations with large meals, while processionals collected food in order to have a small feast of their own. Prayers to Brigid occurred at many points throughout the holiday.

Another Imbolc practice found in coastal areas was to spread seashells in each corner of the home to ensure prosperity via good fishing throughout the year (O Suilleabhain, 1967). In more rural areas efforts were made at Imbolc to protect the cows, and some of the newly woven Brigid's crosses might by hung in the stable as well as the house. In addition, red ribbons or rowan twigs might be tied to the cows' tails or necks (O Suilleabhain, 1967).

A modern devotee of Brigid or anyone seeking to celebrate Imbolc, especially with a group or family, should strive to keep the family-oriented tone of the holiday. One option is to make your own Brigid's crosses, or the small plaques of sun, moon, and stars, as a family and to use a variation of the ritual associated with that activity. Another possibility would be to make a Brideog and invite her in, using a simple ceremony. The eldest daughter, mother, or other appropriate person should be selected to act as Brigid or to carry the Brideog. Going outside, she should knock on the door three times and say something along the lines of, 'Blessed Brigid is here, welcome her in.' To that, the mother or other appropriate person waiting inside should open the door and reply, 'Come in, you are a hundred times welcome.' The brideog should then be shown to its bed and given the slat Brigid, and the family would sit down to dinner with a prayer to Brigid to bless them, possibly using a prayer similar to this one, which is a pagan version based on traditional material:

> *All honor to noble Brigid, and thanks for this meal that we have before us. May we be seven times better off at the end of the year than we find ourselves now. May we have health of body and spirit in our family, wealth and abundance, strength for the year's hardships, protection from fever and diseases. We welcome in blessed Brigid, this day and every day.*[17]

Part of the meal should be ritually offered, in thanks for the Goddess's blessings. In the morning omens can be taken for the coming season and to see if Brigid has blessed the family. In the event that the omens are negative, incense may be burned and an offering made to regain her favor; traditionally the incense would be burned on the hearth and the offering would be buried where three streams meet (Carmichael, 1900).

Imbolc is a holiday that is perfectly tailored for celebration by pagans today who are seeking to honor Brigid. It has always been a holiday of the home and family, with an emphasis on women and girls, and reviving that in modern practice offers a great opportunity to create lasting family traditions as well. Honoring the Goddess Brigid and celebrating the slow return of the warmth and light are things that we can all enjoy and the emphasis on physical actions and on creating objects to use during the ceremonies is also ideal. It is up to each person to decide how explicitly pagan or not to make these practices within their own home, but regardless there are many ways to successfully include Imbolc as a meaningful holiday.

Imbolc – Divination Practices

Divination practices are found during all of the significant Irish celebrations and Imbolc is no exception. The period immediately after the feasting portion of the celebration was often used for divination (Estyn Evans, 1957). In some specific cases relating to the casting of lots for fisherman or the reading of the marks in the ashes, the divination occurred on the morning of the festival (Danaher, 1972). A practice among families is to light a candle representing each family member and watch the order in which they burn out, which will be the same order each person will die in (Wilde, 1991).

Several Imbolc omens relied on seeing certain animals, and sometimes on noting what the animal was doing. Seeing a hedgehog on Imbolc was believed to be an omen of good weather to come, as it was believed that if the hedgehog sensed bad weather coming in the early spring season he would return to his burrow (Danaher, 1972). This seems to be reflected in the

American practice of looking to groundhogs for weather predictions at the same time of year. If you hear a lark singing on Imbolc it is an omen of a good spring (Danaher, 1972).

Weather omens were also very commonly noted. Rain on Imbolc was believed to foreshadow pleasant weather in the coming summer (Danaher, 1972). A windy Imbolc means snow in March (Carmichael, 1900). In the Isle of Man it was believed that snow on Brigid's day meant a fair spring and a sunny Brigid's day meant snow before May 1st (Moore, 1891).

A ritual for divination involved the use of the slat Brighid, or Brigid's wand, a peeled stick made of a white wood that was left with an effigy of Brigid near the hearth overnight. The ashes of the fire would be carefully smoothed when the family went to bed and in the morning the marks of the wand appearing in the ashes were a good omen (Carmichael, 1900). An even better omen was the mark of a footprint, seen as a sign that Brigid herself had visited and blessed the home (Carmichael, 1900). Very unlucky though was the home with no mark left in the ashes at all. To turn this ill omen, incense was burned through the next night on the fireplace and a chicken buried as an offering at the joining of three streams (Carmichael, 1900).

Brigid and Lúnasa

Although Brigid's most well-known holiday is Imbolc she also has stories and myths related to Lúnasa. In a story related in the Bethu Brigte Brigid was called on during a Lúnasa assembly to help settle a legal dispute for saint Patrick when one of his priests was accused of having fathered a child (Patterson, 1994). Brigid miraculously gave the perfect verdict, solving the problem, and echoing her role as Brigid of the Judgments.

An established Lúnasa custom is the visiting and garlanding of holy wells, and this is true for Brigid's holy wells. The tradition today is a Christian one, but we can perhaps see echoes of older pagan traditions, where the community would gather at a sacred well and decorate it with flowers. In modern tradition this is accompanied by formal prayers and a circumambulating of the well three times clockwise for blessing (MacNeill, 1962).

The story of saint Brigid defeating the monstrous Suicín is also sometimes said to have taken place on the Sunday before Lúnasa. In these versions the monster was believed to be either a servant of Crom Dubh or Crom Dubh himself (MacNeill, 1962). This may be a later interpolation of pagan myths where a deity of civilization had to defend or earn the harvest from a force of chaos, although usually these roles are taken by Lugh and Crom Dubh or Lugh and Balor. It is, however, possible that Brigid in this case as a deity of fertility and abundance would have been the local choice in the area that worshiped her to be the defender of the food supply. Maire MacNeill suggests that further studies of local cults of the Cailleach Bhéara, as well as saints Brigid and Ann (Brigid and Anu, perhaps?) may prove insightful for an understanding of the various Goddesses' roles in the harvest festival (MacNeill, 1962).

Brigid in My Life

A Family Imbolc 2014

Imbolc of 2014 was a special one for me, celebrating with the children, for two reasons. Firstly, because my oldest daughter, who was ten at the time, had taken an active interest in participating over that year. Secondly, because I had spent the previous Imbolc in the hospital recovering from a near-fatal postpartum complication after the birth of my son. This Imbolc I was home with my family, healthy, and had my children fully joining in to celebrate our traditions.

Kevin Danaher in his book *The Year in Ireland* explains in detail about different Imbolc celebrations and I take some of my inspiration for practice from him. For example, I start my holiday at sunset on January 31st, Imbolc eve, when it would have been traditional for families to prepare a big dinner, welcome Brigid in, make new Brigid's crosses, and set out a brat Brighid, or Brigid's mantle, for the Goddess to bless when she visited overnight. In the morning omens were looked for to confirm Brigid's blessing on the home, athletic games might be enjoyed and the community would gather to celebrate.

On Imbolc eve we prepared the leaba Bhrighid, Brigid's bed, placing it in front of the fireplace. My oldest daughter took the Brideog (a small doll representing Brigid) outside and knocked on the door, announcing, 'Open the door and let blessed Brigid in!'

Holding the baby, I opened the door with my younger daughter at my side and we said, 'Welcome! Welcome! Welcome! We welcome in Brigid to our home, your bed is ready.'

We all walked up to where the leaba Bhrighid was waiting and placed the Brideog inside, tucking her in and placing a small willow wand, the slat geal, in with the doll.

We sang a little song we made up:

We welcome you in
We welcome you in
We welcome you in
Blessed Brighid is here

Your bed is ready
Your bed is ready
Your bed is ready
Blessed Brighid is here

Please bless our home
Please bless our home
Please bless our home
Blessed Brighid is here

The children really enjoyed the pageantry of it all and especially the singing. I told them a few stories about Brigid and who she was and we talked a little bit about her symbols and the different things, like the leaba Brighid, that we were using. After getting the Brideog set up I placed my brat Brighid out on the windowsill, and we went to bed.

In the morning we woke up to bright sun and mild temperatures. We looked for omens of Brigid's visit and received several positive ones, including the sight of a rare horned lark; larks being birds associated with Brigid, and their song an omen of good weather to come. I also noted the lack of wind, tying into another traditional Imbolc omen:

As far as the wind shall enter the door
On the Feast Day of Bride,
The snow shall enter the door
On the Feast Day of Patrick.
(*Carmina Gadelica*, 1900)

Later that day we made new Brigid's crosses, and we ended our celebration with a dinner of pork and colcannon that night, with a portion offered to the ancestors, aos si, and Brigid herself.

Chapter Five

The Goddess in Modern Times

When softly blew the south wind o'er the sea,
Lisping of springtime hope and summer pride,
And the rough reign of Beira ceased to be,
Angus the Ever-Young,
The beauteous god of love, the golden-haired,
The blue mysterious-eyed,
Shone like the star of morning high among
The stars that shrank afraid
When dawn proclaimed the triumph that he shared
With Bride the peerless maid.
Then winds of violet sweetness rose and sighed,
No conquest is compared
To Love's transcendent joys that never fade.
(MacKenzie, 1917)

Historically we have seen who Brigid was to the pre-Christian pagans as well as how the early Irish, Scottish, and Welsh Christians understood her and how she survived in folk belief. That provides a firm foundation to move forward from, but Brigid in the modern world is more than just an amalgam of her past; she has also formed new stories and new associations in the modern world, which have taken root in the modern pagan community. To truly know Brigid as a Goddess we must see both her history and her present, in order to understand how the two together are shaping her future.

Modern Myths

Ella Young was an Irish poet in the early 20th century who wrote a book called *Celtic Wonder Tales* in 1910 that re-tells the stories of the Irish Gods. Young used her skill as a poet and her background in Theosophy to re-imagine the old myths and blend the old beliefs with new interpretations. There is no surviving Irish creation story, so Young wrote one titled Earth-Shapers, which is the opening chapter of her book, imagining Brigid as the driving force behind the Gods making the earth habitable. In her version earth is a shapeless chaos and the Gods inhabit 'The Land of the Living Heart'; Brigid is so drawn to the void of earth that she can't resist singing to it, which awakens it and draws all the other Gods to her side (Young, 1910). Although the Gods initially tell her to forget the earth she persuades them instead to help her change it from chaos to order, and at her urging they bring the four treasures of the Tuatha Dé Danann.[18] Using the four treasures and Brigid's mantle the Gods make the earth a place of beauty.

Although this myth is entirely modern and departs radically from older folklore in several ways it has become quite popular with some followers of Brigid. People like the poetry that fills Young's writing and many find an appeal in the central role that Brigid is given. In Young's version of creation, Brigid is the driving force, the passion, that impels and inspires all the other Gods to act and to make the earth what it becomes.

A similarly popular modern creation myth was written by Peter Berresford Ellis in his book Celtic Myths and Legends in 1999. Titled the Ever Living Ones, it describes Danu and Bile as cosmic forces, which unite and produce two acorns that birth the Dagda and Brigid. The pair then go on to found the four cities of the Gods and to become the pre-eminent divinities of the pantheon among their children, the Tuatha Dé Danann. The four treasures are mentioned here as well.[19] In the story after an extended amount of time it is the Dagda and Brigid who urge their children to leave the Otherworld and go to earth, and due to the changes it is the Fomorians who first keen for the dead after Ruadán is killed as the story removes Brigid as his mother.

As with Young's story Ellis took liberal poetic liberty, blending older myth with modern imagination to create a hybrid. His version is probably the one I hear most often repeated, in part because many people do not realize his book is not original mythology, but his own fictionalized versions.

Another modern idea that has crept into Brigid's mythology is the identity of her mother. In the older myths her mother is never named; in the life of the Christian saint her mother is a slave. However, modern pagan texts like to say that her mother is either Boínn or the Morrigan. The idea that it might be Boínn is based on two main facts: that Boínn is Óengus's mother and so could potentially also be Brigid's making the two full siblings; and the conflation of saint Brigid as a baby being fed by a white Otherworldly cow and Boínn's own association with white cows.[20] The other school of thought argues that Brigid was the result of the Dagda and the Morrigan uniting at Samhain before the battle with the Fomorians, or otherwise being a product of a union between those two.

Personally I am skeptical of the second idea, because Brigid is never listed anywhere as the Morrigan's daughter and she was not only clearly alive before the battle with the Fomorians, but was an adult with a grown son when that war happened. It also seems unlikely since Brigid is conflated with the Morrigan in the *Lebor Gabala Erenn*, although in fairness that conflation also has serious issues that make it unlikely which were discussed in the first chapter. I can see the logic of seeing Boínn as her mother, however, particularly if we view the story of the saint's life as a reflection of older mythology of the Goddess. However, the reader is free to decide for themselves; both ideas are popular today and neither can be proven.

Some people today choose to see Brigid as a triple Goddess in the modern sense of the Maiden, Mother, and Crone. Where she is placed in this schema varies, but I have seen her as both the Maiden and the Mother in other people's systems. Drawing on the works of authors like Robert Graves and Fiona McLeod/William Sharp some modern pagans have put aside Brigid's mythic history and chosen to focus on her presence as depicted in the poetry and modern prose of the last century.[21] From this viewpoint Brigid's motherly and inspirational aspects are built up and her martial and agricultural aspects are diminished or ignored; she becomes a Goddess of the suburban hearth and home and of the digital poet's keyboard. Brigid as a healing Goddess remains a major focus though, but without the emphasis on childbirth and livestock it once held in folk tradition.

Modern Flame Tending

The perpetual flame at Brigid's church in Kildare was thought to have burned until the 16th century. In 1993 the flame was relit by the Catholic Brigadine sisters and has been tended at Kildare since then. Another modern pagan practice for Brigid also involves flame tending, which can be done as part of international non-denominational Orders, as part of smaller pagan groups that include the practice, or on an individual basis. Modern flametending generally follows the same approach that ancient flametending was believed to have used, with 19 women – or men in those groups that allow mixed gender flametending – taking a day each tending her fire, usually represented in this case by a candle flame. On the 20th day Brigid is said to tend her own fire.

Offerings

Offerings to Brigid could include milk, butter, cheese, bread, and in some cases chicken.[22] Beer and ale would also be appropriate, especially those brewed from malt. For a modern practitioner these would all still be viable options and reflect Brigid's connection to agriculture and dairy products. I've also personally made offerings of things I've made, either physical craft items or of poems for example, usually by burning them. Traditionally offerings to Brigid would be left out, often on windowsills on Imbolc, for example, with the understanding that it was a blessing omen should the offering be taken and eaten by anything (or anyone). As a general rule of thumb for myself I will place an offering on my altar and leave it overnight, in order for the substance to be consumed, and then dispose of the remains the next day.

Altars

Making an altar to Brigid is a good way to begin connecting to her, and there are a variety of ways to approach this. Exactly what is on a modern altar and how the altar is used can vary widely, but generally each tradition or faith will have guidelines or expectations for the set-up of an altar. Most altars that I have seen will include sacred images, candles, and a place or bowl for offerings, but some may also include a variety of objects and tools. My own altars tend to get very elaborate as I try to include a variety of things that are important to me, but I have seen some that are as simple as a candle and incense burner.

For people who like statues there are a variety of good ones on the market now, from museum replicas by companies like Sacred Source to modern depictions like those by Dryad Design. There are also a huge variety of paintings and 2-D artwork to choose from, many of them made by pagan artists who are approaching depicting Brigid as a sacred act. I provide a short annotated list of possible sources in the appendix for anyone interested.

For those who aren't comfortable using an image to represent Brigid on their altar there are other options. Some people choose to use objects that symbolize her or something she is strongly associated with. Perhaps a smith's anvil or hammer for Brigid of Smithcraft, or a mortar and pestle to represent Brigid as Goddess of healing. Another option is a simple candle or even a stone to represent her.

Guided Meditation to Brigid

Another more esoteric way to connect to Brigid that can work really well, especially if you like meditation work, is doing a guided meditation. You can do this yourself by memorizing the script of the meditation or you can do it with help by having someone else read it to you.

Find somewhere quiet where you can sit or lie down comfortably. Once you are comfortable close your eyes and take three slow, deep breaths.

You are surrounded by white light; it purifies and protects you.

Visualize yourself in a familiar safe place. A path opens up in front of you, lined with trees; when you are ready start to walk down the path. Feel the earth cool beneath your feet. The branches of oak and rowan weave together on each side of you forming a tunnel of trees. The sun is high overhead, the light filtering down through the leaves. As you walk you realize that the trees are thinning ahead of you, opening up to a field.

Step out of the tunnel of trees and off the path. In front of you stretches a wide field that looks like it may have been a pasture for animals once. The sun is hot, warming the grass beneath your feet, and the air is heavy with the smell of hay and the distant sound of sheep and cows. Across the field you see a small house sitting alone on a slight rise in the land. Smoke curls from its chimney and you can see a few chickens wandering lazily in front of the doorway.

You walk slowly across the field, enjoying the feeling of peace that hangs in the air. The blue sky above you and the green world around you have a timeless quality, as if they have always existed just like this and always will. Even though you have never been here before there is something familiar and comforting about everything. When you reach the house you pause for a moment and study the building, looking at its shape and color. The door is open and after a moment you hear a woman's voice calling out to you, inviting you in.

You walk through the door and find a welcoming room, with a woman waiting for you inside. 'I am Brigid, welcome to my home. I have been waiting for you,' she says.

She smiles as you look around the room, your eyes taking in the variety of objects it contains. When you are done studying the room you turn to look at the figure standing before you, who is waiting patiently. When you have gotten accustomed to everything she speaks again, 'You have come here seeking me, as many do. Am I what you expected?'

You answer her honestly. She nods, then says, 'Is there a question you wish to ask me?'

If you have a question you may ask Brigid now and she answers.

After she has told you what you need to know, she hands you a token to take back with you and asks you to leave something with her as an offering. You hand her whatever you most want to give to the Goddess. Thank her for speaking with you, then politely leave the house. Make your way back across the field and to the path at the edge of the woods. Walk into the forest, down the path with the trees surrounding you.

As you walk through the trees the light fades as the branches above you block the sun. The ground is cool beneath your feet. You breathe deeply and listen to the rustle of leaves surrounding you. As you walk down the tunnel of trees you feel the sense of peace that you felt in the Goddess's house still filling you. You know that you are protected and you carry her blessing with you. You move forward and see in front of you the trees opening up, delivering you back to the place you began. You step back into your safe place, your starting place. You are surrounded by white light. Take three deep breaths, slowly in through your nose and out through your mouth. Feel the ground beneath your body. Breathe in, and out. You are back fully in your body now, take a moment to stretch and settle yourself before opening your eyes.

If you have a journal, immediately after the meditation is a good time to write down any experiences you had.

Brigid in My Life

I had a very bad head cold the week before a major weekend pagan event that I was scheduled to attend and teach workshops at as well as assisting in a major ritual on the second night. I was sick enough that I debated not going to the event at all, but in the end I decided to load up on medication, cough drops, and tissue and try to tough it out rather than fail in a commitment I had made. I taught my class that Friday afternoon with the aid of lots of Dayquil and sheer willpower.

That Friday night I went to a Brigid ritual, which featured the chance to face three faces of Brigid, if people wanted to. I chose to face them. I will say there was, for me, a lot of Macha in facing Brigid, but that's a bit of a different story. As we sat in the circle I was still feeling distinctly ill, but also strongly motivated to participate. The priestess leading the ritual explained that three people, seated on a central dias which normally served as a raised fire circle, had taken on the roles of Brigid of the Forge, Brigid of the Well, and Brigid of the Poets. Those who chose to approach them were asked to form a line and by whatever fluke or synchronicity I ended up at the head of the line. The first Brigid asked me a question and I answered. I went to the second Brigid, Brigid of the Well, who also asked me a question. Then there was a point where I had water poured on my head and she put her hand over my collarbone. I felt an intense energy go through me, and had a hard time grounding for a while afterwards (enough that several people asked me if I was okay).

From that moment on, I was not sick.

The entire rest of the weekend I never again took any

medication and felt completely fine, besides the usual over-tiredness from lack of sleep.

After leaving Brigid of the Well I walked to the final Brigid and then returned to my seat, in a state I can only describe as euphoric. As I mentioned several people asked me repeatedly if I was alright and the strange thing is, I was. The difference in my health was profound and noticeable, enough that many people who attended the same event have and will vouch that what I am saying is true – at least that I was very sick when I arrived and was perfectly healthy after the Brigid ritual. Enough that instead of going to bed early as I'd planned I ended up going to the post-ritual party and staying up rather late, and had no issues teaching the next day or with the Macha ritual I was helping with.

Nothing like this has ever happened to me before, and I found it rather...complex to process. I'm still not sure exactly what I think about, but I want to share the experience. You can decide for yourself what you think of it.

Chapter Six

Prayers, Chants, and Charms

We will take the Sword of Light,' said Brigit, 'and the Cauldron of Plenty and the Spear of Victory and the Stone of Destiny with us, for we will build power and wisdom and beauty and lavish-heartedness into the Earth.

'It is well said,' cried all the Shining Ones.
(Young, 1910)

Prayers are an important way to connect to Gods we honor. As meditation is a way to listen to the Gods, praying is a way to speak to them. For some people prayer will only be used in a ritual context while for others prayer can be a daily practice as part of devotional work. If one is willing to modify Christian prayers for use in a pagan context then there is an extensive number of prayers to Brigid to draw on; however, modern pagan prayers to Brigid are rapidly increasing as well. This chapter will include a variety of traditional prayers and chants, modern prayers, as well as a selection of magical charms calling on Brigid for different purposes.

(Original Scottish Gaidhlig) Slionntireachd Bhride

Slionneadh na Ban-naomh Bride,
Lasair dhealrach oir, muime chorr Chriosda.
Bride nighinn Dughaill duinn,
Mhic Aoidh, mhic Airt, nitric Cuinn,
Mhic Crearair, mhic Cis, mhic Carmaig, mhic Carruinn.

Gach la agus gach oidhche
Ni mi sloinntireachd air Bride,
Cha mharbhar mi, cha spuillear mi,

Cha charcar mi, cha chiurar mi,
Cha mhu dh' fhagas Criosd an dearmad mi.

Cha loisg teine, grian, no gealach mi,
Cha bhath luin, li, no sala mi,
Cha reub saighid sithich, no sibhich mi,
Is mi fo chomaraig mo Naomh Muire
Is i mo chaomh mhuime Bride.

The genealogy of the holy maiden Bride,
Radiant flame of gold, noble foster-mother of Christ,
Bride the daughter of Dugall the brown,
Son of Aodh, son of Art, son of Conn,
Son of Crearar, son of Cis, son of Carina, son of Carruin.

Every day and every night
That I say the genealogy of Bride,
I shall not be killed, I shall not be harried,
I shall not be put in cell, I shall not be, wounded,
Neither shall Christ leave me in forgetfulness.

No fire, no sun, no moon shall burn me,
No lake, no water, nor sea shall drown mc,
No arrow of fairy nor dart of fay shall wound me,
And I under the protection of my Holy Mary,
And my gentle foster-mother is my beloved Bride.
(Carmichael, 1900)

Genealogy of Brighid (Pagan Version)
The genealogy of the holy goddess Brighid,
Radiant flame of gold, noble mother of Ruadan,
Brighid, the daughter of an Daghda the Good God,
Brighid, daughter of Boanne, shining white,
Every day and every night

That I say the genealogy of Brighid,
I shall not be killed, I shall not be harried,
I shall not be jailed , I shall not be wounded,
Nor shall my Gods leave me.
No fire, no sun, no moon shall burn me,
No lake, no water, nor sea shall drown mc,
No arrow of fairy nor dart of Fey shall wound me,
I am under the protection of the Gods of life,
And my gentle foster-mother is my beloved Brighid.
(Modified based on material from volume 1 of the *Carmina Gadelica*)

Modern Prayer to Brigid for a Good Childbirth

There came to my assistance,
Blessed fair Brigid;
As you bore Rúadan,
As Boínn bore Óengus,
As Eithne bore Lugh the many-skilled
Without a blemish on him,
Aid me in my bearing,
Aid me, O Brigid!

As Lugh was conceived of Eithne
Full perfect on every hand,
Assist me, Brigid, aid-woman,
The conception to bring from the bone;
As you have aided so many generations before me,
Without gold, without corn, without kine,
May you aid me, for great is my distress,
Aid me, O Brigid!
(Modified based on material from volume 1 of the *Carmina Gadelica*)

Invocation to Brighid (the Poet)

Noble Lady of inspiration
Blessed Brighid of the poets
Inspiring Lady
I call to you

Invocation of Brighid (of the Forge)

Blessed Brighid of the forge
Creator, transformer,
Who shapes raw material
Into form and function
I call to you

Invocation to Brighid (the Healer)

Brighid of the healing well,
Brighid of the healing cloak
Brighid of the healing word
I call to you

Travel Prayer to Brigid Brigiu

Brigid of the Hostel
Lady of warm welcomes
She who provides for all
Who feeds the hungry
And shelters the traveler
I am a wanderer today
Far from home, far from my kin
Let me find a welcome
In these strange lands
May your spirit shine
Through those around me
Brigid of many welcomes
Be with me where ever I go

Prayer to Brigid of the Judgments

Lady of Judges
Fair minded one
Who always gives
Just rulings
May you speak
Truth for my case
May you bring justice
To my cause
Brigid of the Judgments
May you prevail

Offering Prayer to Brigid Ambue

I call to the Lady of the Outsiders
I call to the Lady of the Foreigners
I call to the Lady of the Voiceless
You protect those who society rejects
You guard those who need guarding
You speak for those without power
I honor you, great lady of the cowless
I honor your peerless integrity
I honor your courage and conviction
Accept this offering I give you

Mourning Prayer

Ochon! A Bhrighid!
My heart is breaking
My grief is boundless
O Brigid, mourning mother
I cannot contain this sadness
Ochon! A Bhrighid!
My heart is broken
Death has taken my love
O Brigid, keening woman

I am weeping. I am wailing
Ochon! A Bhrighid!
My tears are a river
Washing my soul
O Brigid, comfort-giver
Help me find strength

The following consist of magical folk charms which call on Brigid to help with a particular situation. She is often called on in folk magic for healing and for protection, sometimes with actions accompanying the spoken charm.

Prayer to Brigit to Heal a Toothache

The incantation put by lovely Brigit
Before the thumb of the Mother of the Gods,
On lint, on wort, on hemp,
For worm, for venom, for teeth.

The worm that tortured me,
In the teeth of my head,
Pain hard by my teeth,
The teeth painfully distressing me.

The teeth healed in my mouth;
As long as I myself shall last
May my teeth last in my head.

Variants:

On lint, on comb, on agony.
On sea, on ocean, on coast.
On water, on lakes, on marshes.
(Modified from material found in the *Carmina Gadelica*)

A Healing Chant Using a Crystal

This charm is traditionally done using a clear quartz healing stone and water from one of Brigid's healing wells, but it can be modified for use with any stone or water. The crystal would be dipped into water, while the person chanted:

> Let me dip thee in the water
> Thou yellow, beautiful gem of power!
> In water of purest wave,
> Which Bridget didn't permit to be contaminated.
> In the name of the Apostles twelve,
> In the name of Mary, Virgin of virtues,
> And in the name of the High Trinity
> And all the shining angels,
> A blessing on the gem,
> A blessing in the water, and
> A healing of bodily ailments to each suffering creature.
> (Black, 1894)

For my own purposes I prefer to use a slightly different version:

> Let me dip you in the water
> You beautiful gem of power!
> In water of purest wave,
> Which Brighid kept pure.
> A blessing on the gem,
> A blessing in the water, and
> A healing of bodily ailments
> to each suffering creature.

Against the Evil Eye

This is a modified version of a folk charm that tradition says was used by saint Brigid to protect from and remove the evil eye:

If a fairy, or a man, or a woman has overlooked you,
There are three greater who will cast evil from you,
Into the great and terrible sea,
Pray to them, and they will watch over you.[23]

The following is an entirely traditional Scottish charm to Saint Brigid for protection on animals, especially livestock. It comes from volume 2 of the *Carmina Gadelica*, a work that is truly a treasure trove of old prayers and folk charms.

Sian Bride (Scottish Gaidhlig)

Sian a chuir Bride nam buadh,
M'a mise, m'a cire, m'a buar,
M'a capuill, m'a cathmhil, m'a cual,
Moch is anamach dol dachaidh is uaith.

Gan cumail bho chreagan, bho chleitean,
Bho ladhara 's bho adhaircean a cheile,
Bho iana na Creige Ruaidh,
Is bho Luath na Feinne.

Bho lannaire liath Creag Duilionn,
Bho iolaire riabhach Beinn-Ard,
Bho sheobhag luth Torr-an-Duin,
Is fitheach dur Creag-a-Bhaird.

Bho mhada-ruadh nan cuireid,
Bho mhada-ulai a Mhaim,
Bho thaghan tocaidh na tuide,
'S bho mhaghan udail a mhais.
Bho gach ceithir-chasach spuireach,
Agus guireach da sgiath.
(Carmicheal, 1900)

Saint Brigid's Charm

The charm put by Bride the beneficent,
On her goats, on her sheep, on her kine,
On her horses, on her chargers, on her herds,
Early and late going home, and from home.

To keep them from rocks and ridges,
From the heels and the horns of one another
From the birds of the Red Rock,
And from Luath of the Feinne.

From the blue peregrine hawk of Creag Duilion,
From the brindled eagle of Ben-Ard,
From the swift hawk of Tordun,
From the surly raven of Bard's Creag.

From the fox of the wiles,
From the wolf of the Mam,
From the foul-smelling fumart,
And from the restless great-hipped bear.
From every hoofed of four feet,
And from every hatched of two wings.

Brigid in My Life

I have an altar to Brigid in my house that has slowly been built up over many years of honoring her. The centerpiece is a statue of the three Brigids, the healer, poet, and smith; a Dryad Design product it really captures the essence of the deities for me. To make the statue more personal I painted it, choosing colors for each of the three images that best resonated with my own feelings for each of the three daughters of the Dagda. Around the statue I have included objects that I associate with the three sisters as well: a clay whistle shaped like a bodhrán, which I made in high school, a mortar and pestle filled with a selection of herbs, and a special candle. The candle is red and I made it by filling it with herbs and dressing it with oils chosen for Brigid of the forge. I also keep my brat Bhride there and a bottle that holds water from Brigid's well in Kildare. In front of the altar is a small brass cauldron, and whenever someone is sick or in need of healing I write their name down and then put it into this cauldron to petition Brigid to help them.

When someone is sick in the house I also bring out my brat Bhride to put over them, and if it seems particularly bad I may dip my healing stone in some of the water from her well, chant the charm to her for blessing the stone mentioned previously, and use that as well. My middle child has several chronic medical issues so Brigid is a regular presence in our home. If someone's name has been put into her cauldron for healing, when they are feeling better the paper is burned and some ghee or butter is offered in thanks.

Conclusion

Brigid is a complex and fascinating deity who in many ways exists in the liminal place between the pagan past and present. Her roots reach back into the distant past, beyond Irish myth and into a place where only hints and guesses of her origins remain. For more than a millennia she blended and blurred into the Catholic saint of the same name, so deeply that even the best scholars today are left unsure of where exactly one ends and the other begins. In modern paganism Brigid emerges as an amalgam of all of this, weaving together older pagan myths, Christian beliefs, and new pagan beliefs into a thoroughly modern Goddess. Carmichael referred to her as the 'Mary and the Juno of the Gael', and this may perfectly describe the union of Goddess and saint that we see in Brigid (McNeill, 1959). She is both, and in a way she isn't exactly either, existing in the liminal space between each.

We can say a great deal about Brigid with certainty and yet we can know very little about her for certain. She is one of the Tuatha Dé Danann, yet she may have come to Ireland from Gaul as late as the 1st century, and then spread from Ireland to Scotland and Wales 600 years later in the guise of a Catholic saint. She is a Goddess of healing, but also of warfare and landless warriors, a Goddess of poets and law-speakers and a defender of those who have no legal standing. She is a Goddess of heights and of rivers, of sacred water and of flame. She is the sovereignty of Leinster, wife of a divine king and owner of kingly animals. She is the mother of outlawed sons who die by violence, and she is a virgin saint who is mother to all who pray to her, midwife and foster-mother to the son of a foreign God who also died by violence.

Brigid's strength has always been her versatility. She is a Goddess who appeals to all people, at all levels of society, who fills roles that at one point or another we will all need help with. She understands our joy at the birth of a child and she understands our mourning at the death of a loved one. Hers is the flame that reshapes and molds us, hers is the water that cleanses and blesses us, hers is the bounty of the earth and the livestock upon it that sustains us. And hers is the pounding hammer of the forge that creates both tools of agriculture and weapons of war to support and protect us.

As long as there are people who seek her, she will be there, waiting to be found, waiting to be remembered.

Appendix A: Pronunciation

Brigid is a widely popular Goddess and her name appears across multiple cultures in various forms; because of this there are several different ways to spell and say her name. I'm going to include a variety of different forms and pronunciations here for readers to get an idea of possible ways to approach her name.

Old Irish
Bric or Brig – BRIHG

Modern Irish
Brighid or Bríd – BREEJ / BREEDJ
Anglicized to Bridgit or Bridgid – Brih-jihd

Welsh
Ffraid – Frait

Scottish Gaidhlig
Bride or Brighde – BREE-dja

Manx
Breeshey – Bree-JUH

Gaulish
Brigandu – brig-UHN-du
Brigindu – brig-IN-du
Briga – BRIG-ah

Appendix B: Mixed Media Resources

Because Brigid is a Goddess of poets and inspiration I feel it's important to include a list of mixed media related to her. We can experience her not only in non-fiction texts, but also in fiction, in song, and artwork. And not only can we, but perhaps more than any other deity we should.

This list is, of course, only a small sample of suggestions.

Fiction
The Book of Kells by R. A. MacAvoy
Priestess of the Fire Temple by Ellen Evert Hopmen
The Iron Druid Chronicles (series) by Kevin Hearne
Celtic Wonder Tales by Ella Young
The Hounds of the Morrigan by Pat O'Shea

Music
Brighid's Flame by Kellianna off of her CD Elemental
Brighid by Kellianna off her CD Lady Moon
Brigid by Jenna Greene off her CD Wild Earth Child
Brighid's Kiss by La Lugh off the CD Brighid's Kiss
Brighid by Damh the Bard off his CD Antlered Crown and
    Standing Stone
Brighid of the Sacred Flame by Angela Little from the CD Celtic
    Flame
Song to Brighid by Lisa Theil of her CD Song for My Ancestors

Statues
Sacred Source has an entire page on its website dedicated to
    Brigid: http://www.sacredsource.com/Brigid/products/61/
Dryad Design has a gorgeous statue depicting the three
    daughters of the Dagda:
    http://dryaddesign.com/brigid-statue/

Artwork

Ashley Bryner has as series of pictures featuring different aspects of Brigid (including the one featured on the cover of this book) that can be found for sale on Etsy here
https://www.etsy.com/shop/lindowyn

Artist Jane Brideson has a beautiful piece titled Brighid which can be found on her website
http://theeverlivingones.blogspot.com/p/gallery-of-goddesses.html

Hrana Janto includes a beautiful image of Brighid in her Goddess Oracle deck
http://www.thegoddessoracle.com/brigid.htm

Jo Jayson has an evocative image of Brighid available as a series of prints
https://www.etsy.com/listing/151292522/brighid-mother-goddess-of-ireland?ref=shop_home_active_1&ga_search_ query=Brighid

Other Sources

Besides finding Brigid in different forms of media, we can also find her through other people's eyes online, in websites and blogs and different organizations. Of course these sources will have a variety of different viewpoints and not all will agree; I recommend using the information found so far in this book as a measuring stick to judge information found elsewhere, but keep in mind that modern interpretations of the Goddess are often very personal and may be more or less based on actual history and myth depending on the person or group.

Websites and Blogs

Brigit's Sparkling Flame
http://brigitssparklingflame.blogspot.com/

Brigit's Forge
http://www.brigitsforge.co.uk/

Brigid, Goddess and Saint
http://brighid.org.uk/index.html

Virtual Shrine of Brighid
http://www.celticheritage.co.uk/virtualshrine/

Brighid, Bright Goddess of the Gael
http://www.imbas.org/articles/brighid.html

Loop of Brighid
http://www.patheos.com/blogs/agora/2013/01/what-is-brigidine-paganism/

Also (Specifically focusing on the Christian aspects of Candlemas, but exceptionally well researched) Redeeming Holy Days Candlemas Presentation
http://steadfastlutherans.org/2015/01/redeeming-holy-days-candlemaspresentation-2/

Organizations
Ord Brighideach International
http://www.ordbrighideach.org/raven/

Daughters of the Flame
http://www.obsidianmagazine.com/DaughtersoftheFlame/

Bibliography

Anderson, G., (2008). *Birds of Ireland: Facts, Folklore & History*

Baring-Gould, S., and Fisher, J., (1913) *Lives of the British Saints*

Beith, M., (1995) *Healing Threads: Traditional Medicines of the Highlands and Islands*

Borsje, J., (2012). Love Magic in Medieval Irish Penitentials, Law, and Literature

Black, G., (1894). *Scottish Charms and Amulets*

Carmichael, A., (1900). *Carmina Gadelica* volume 1

Clark, R., (1991). *The Great Queens: Irish Goddesses from the Morrigan to Cathleen ní Houlihan_*

Daimler, M., (2015). *The Treasure of the Tuatha Dé Danann: A dual language collection of Irish myth*

Danaher, K., (1972). *The Year in Ireland*

eDIL (n.d.). electronic Dictionary of the Irish Language

Ellis, P., (1987). *A Dictionary of Irish Mythology*

Ellis, P., (1994). *Dictionary of Celtic Mythology*

Ellis, P., (1999). *Celtic Myths and Legends*

Estyn Evans, E., (1957). *Irish Folk Ways*

Gray, E., (1983). *Cath Maige Tuired*

Green, M., (1995). *Celtic Goddesses*

Green, M., (1992). *Dictionary of Celtic Myth and Legend*

Guyonvarc'h, C., (1999). *The Making of a Druid; Hidden Teachings from the Colloquy of Two Sages*

Keifer, D., (2001). Brewing: a Legacy of Ancient Times. Retrieved from http://pubs.acs.org/subscribe/archive/tcaw/10/i12/html/12chemchron.html

Kelly, F., (1988). *A Guide to Early Irish Law*

Lehmann, R., and Lehmann, W., (1975). *An Introduction to Old Irish*

MacAlister, R., (1941). *Lebor Gabála Érenn*. Part IV

MacDevitt, W., (2009). *The Gallic Wars*

MacKenzie, D., (1917). *Wonder Tales From Scottish Myth and Legend*

MacKillop, J., (1998). *A Dictionary of Celtic Mythology*

Mahon, M., (1919). *Ireland's Fairy Lore*

McCone, K., (2000). *Pagan Past and Christian Present in Early Irish Literature*

McCormick, F., (2008). The Decline of the Cow: Agricultural and Settlement Change in Early Medieval Ireland

McCormick, F., (2010). Ritual Feasting in Iron Age Ireland. Retrieved from https://www.qub.ac.uk/schools/gap/Staff/FileStore/Filetoupload,287068,en.pdf

McIntyre, M., (2015). The Cailleach Bheara: a Study of Scottish Highland Folklore in Literature and Film. Retrieved from https://www.academia.edu/6088609/The_Cailleach_Bheara_A_Study_of_Scottish_Highland_Folklore_in_Literature_and_Film

McNeill, F., (1956). *The Silver Bough*, volume 1

McNeill, F., (1959). *The Silver Bough*, volume 2

Meyer, K., (1890). Tochmarc Emire, Revue Celtique XI

Meyer, K., (1894). *Hibernica Minora*

Meyer, K., (1906). *Triads of Ireland*

Meyer, K., (1912). 'Hail Brigit' an Old Irish Poem on the Hill of Alenn

Monaghan, P., (2004). *The Encyclopedia of Celtic Mythology and Folklore*

Moore, A., (1891). *Folklore of the Isle of Man*

O Cathasaigh, T., (2014). *Coire Sois*

O Duinn, S., (2002). *Where Three Streams Meet*

O Duinn, S., (2005). *The Rites of Brigid Goddess and Saint*

O hOgáin, D., (2006). *The Lore of Ireland*

O Suilleabhain, S., (1967). *Nosanna agus Piseoga na nGael*

Patterson, N., (1994). *Cattle Lords & Clansmen*

Puhvel, J., (1987). *Comparative Mythology*

Quin, E., (1983). *Dictionary of the Irish Language Based Mainly on Old and Middle Irish Materials*

Ross, A., (1967). *Pagan Celtic Britain*

Ross, A., (1970). *Pagan Celts*

Ross, A., (1976). *The Folklore of the Scottish Highlands*

Sanas Cormaic (n.d.) Retrieved from http://www.asnc.cam.ac.uk/irishglossaries/

Sjoestedt, M., (1940). *Celtic Gods and Heroes*

Skye, M., (2007). *Goddess Alive*

Theirling, I., (2001). More Then Winter's Crone. Retrieved from http://brigitssparklingflame.blogspot.com/2009/04/more-than-winters-crone-cailleach-in.html

Thompson, C., (2014). The Three Brigids of the *Ulster Cycle* and the Forgotten Origins of Neopagan Theology. Retrieved from http://www.patheos.com/blogs/sermonsfromthemound/2014/11/the-three-brigits-of-the-ulster-cycle-and-the-forgotten-origins-of-neopagan-theology/

Waddell, J., (2014). *Archaeology and Celtic Myth*

Wilde, E., (1991). *Irish Cures, Mystic Charms & Superstitions*

Wolf, C., (2015). The Mythical Pairing of Brig and Bres – Its Origin and Meaning in *Cath Maige Tuired*. Retrieved from https://www.academia.edu/15429641/The_Mythical_Pairing_of_Brig_and_Bres_Its_Origins_and_Meaning_in_Cath_Maige_Tuired_Revised_

Young, E., (1910). *Celtic Wonder Tales*

Endnotes

1. Entire books have been written on the subject of Brigid as both Goddess and saint, like Sean O Duinn's *The Rites of Brigid: Goddess and Saint,* and truly the subject is far too involved for this short introductory text. However, we will touch on it briefly and in the chapter which discusses Brigid's special holiday of Imbolc many traditions which come from folk practices related explicitly to Saint Brigid will be included, on the belief that they do reflect older pagan practices.

2. Celtic is a term used in fields such as anthropology and archaeology to denote cultural groups related by language and art. Historically the Celts included a wide array of tribal groups and nations found across Europe, some of which, like the Gauls and Picts, did not survive to our time period. In the modern era there are six living Celtic nations and these include: Ireland, Scotland, Wales, Cornwall, the Isle of Man, and Brittany. Brigid is found in all of them, either as a pagan Goddess or in her later guise as a Catholic saint, although the evidence for her in the Isle of Man is brief and limited to her name and feast day as a saint, and in Cornwall is only hinted at in the existence of a holy well dedicated to her.

3. Although it should also be noted that the argument for Danu and the Morrigan being the same deity is somewhat more persuasive, but far from conclusive. I discuss this in more depth in *Pagan Portals: The Morrigan.*

4. Ruadán is an interesting but obscure character. His name is usually understood to mean 'red-haired man' but may mean 'little redness' or 'little bloody' or depending on how the word is taken apart we can also get 'fiery red' or 'driving red'; however, if we take his name as beginning

with a verb the meaning could be 'arrival of fate'. Rua is the third person singular future tense of do-roic, meaning 'comes, arrives'; dáin is the genitive of dán which is a really complex word, but includes meanings of fate and destiny. This is purely supposition but is interesting given his role in the *Cath Maige Tuired*.

Also of particular interest, given Bres's connections to the harvest and Brigid's own connections to abundance and brewing the word 'rúadán' with an accent on the first u is a word that means both brownish red and is a name for a type of wheat, emmer, which is used in making malt for brewing.

5. Casey Wolf explores this idea in greater depth in the paper The Mythical Pairing of Brig and Bres – It's Origin and Meaning in *Cath Maige Tuired* and does argue persuasively for Brigid as a sovereignty Goddess based on her influence over the many aspects of human endeavor and prosperity as well as the archetypal pattern in Irish myth and pseudo-history of the king needing to marry the Goddess of sovereignty in order to secure his right to rule. In this aspect at least Brigid's marriage to Bres and their production of a son seems to follow the expected pattern; the subsequent death of their son may in itself be interpreted as portentous of Bres's loss of sovereignty and inevitable loss of the war he starts to try to keep his kingship by force.

6. During the process of making malt the barley or wheat is first soaked until germination begins, and then heated (Keifer, 2001). When metal is being forged it is often repeatedly heated in fire and then cooled in water.

7. Kine is an archaic term for a group of cows.

8. If we look at the Irish material, specifically the Brehon Laws and Senchus Mar, we find laws against a man using 'aipthi' (spoken or physical charms) to gain a wife. A quote from the Senchus Mar tells us:

A Woman to Whom Her companion Gives a Charm when Soliciting Her, so That He Brings Her to Lust
i.e. when he is entreating her, it is then that he gives/utters the charms/spells to press his love upon her; i.e. bride price and éric-fine, according to the nature of the type of charm/spell; it was before entering the law of marriage that the charms/spells were given/uttered to her and it was in the law of marriage that they came to/against her (?) .... and the smacht-fine applicable to the marriage contract from him for it, and bride price and honour-price and body-fine to her; and separation from him; or éric-fine, according to the nature of the type of charm/spell and her choice to her whether it is mutual separation that she will do or it is in the law of marriage that she will be. (Borsje, 2012).

This is reinforced in the Brehon Laws where marriage through seduction by sorcery is listed as one of the acceptable reasons for a woman to divorce her husband (Kelly, 1988). It shows how seriously seduction by sorcery was taken that it was grounds for divorce for a woman, since the other reasons focused entirely on either failure of the man to provide her a child through assorted reasons or the man damaging her honor through slander or physical maiming. That makes the use of such a charm by saint Brigid especially fascinating.

9. Sreth immais, literally 'ordering inspiration' is a technical term in poetry for connecting all words in a verse-line using alliteration. Immais is the genetive singular form of the word imbas. It is likely, in my opinion, that this triad refer to the speech of poets specifically. Also note that ochán which is given here as 'inciting' actually means lamenting or groaning but appears to imply urging a king to battle through lamentation. (The usual terms for inciting would be gressacht or laíded).

10. Transgressions in this case refers to violations of right order. The word used in Old Irish, 'imarbus' (a form of immarmus) is often understood to reference sin, particularly original sin or the fall from grace in Christian doctrine. This should make it clear that what is being discussed here is not a simple transgression, but a moral one of a significant nature.

11. The exact same words are used in Old Irish to describe Brigid's noises when she mourns her son and the noises the animals make when 'transgressions' occur in Ireland – gol 'lamentation' or as a verb golaid 'weeping', 'wailing' and eigem – 'screaming' 'crying in alarm' and also the sound she's said to invent as a warning signal at night – fet – is the same whistling sound the animals make as well. So when Ireland is violated with transgressions the three animals keen for the land as Brigid keened for her son. I believe that this can be seen as reflecting the idea of Brigid as a sovereignty Goddess who embodies the land itself, so that transgressions against the land are violations of the Goddess herself which cause her tutelary animals to keen for her in the exact same manner she mourned her child.

12. It is extremely important when reading this passage in English to understand that the text is *not* saying that Brigid and Danu are the same Goddess. In old Irish the line 'tri de dana', which is given here by Guyonvarc'h as three Gods of Dana, can more likely be read as three Gods of skill or art, particularly since the text immediately states that their mother is Brigid. Dana is the genitive case form of the word dán which has meanings including skill, art, profession, and ability.

13. An entire book could be written about the Cailleach and her complex mythology which is found in both Ireland and Scotland. She is a powerful and primal Goddess whose roots are lost to time, almost certainly being pre-Celtic in

origin. Her name is not a proper name at all but a word borrowed from the Latin pallium meaning veiled or cloaked; when it was taken into the insular Celtic language branches the p shifted to a c, hence palli became cailli in Irish, retaining the same meaning as the Latin word. It also came to be used to mean nun, hag, witch, and generally applied to women in a derogatory sense. The Cailleach then, is literally the 'Hag', the embodiment of cold and storms and the winter half of the year over which she rules, while Bride, the fair Goddess of blessing, healing, and childbirth, rules over the summer.

14. The shift from February 13th back to February 1st occurred when the calendar was changed from the Julian to the Gregorian. This change involved removing 12 days from the calendar in use at that time to re-align and account for the lack of leap years that had cause significant shifting of the dates forward over many centuries. However, the calendar change was not accepted by everyone and especially the common folk in some areas refused to acknowledge the date changes. Because of this in some very rural areas of Ireland and the British Isles the Fire Festivals including Imbolc are still celebrated on the 12th or 13th respectively.

15. The older name for Imbolc is Oimelc a word that literally means 'sheep's milk' from oí – sheep and melg – milk. This is entirely in line with the holiday's strong dairy associations. The *Sanas Cormac* tells us 'Óimelc .i. oi-meug .i. isi aimser andsin tic ass cairach melg .i. ass arinni mblegar..' – Oimelc that is sheep's-milk that is it is that time when milk is suitable for milking, that is milk with regard to milking. The etymology of Imbolc is uncertain and contested.

16. Midsummer was Áine's special holy day and up until the 19th century people continued to celebrate her on the eve of Midsummer with a procession around her hill, Cnoc Áine,

carrying torches of burning straw in honor of Áine na gClair, Áine of the Wisps, who it was believed returned on that night to visit with and bless her people (Ellis, 1987; O Duinn, 2002). Áine is also sometimes called Áine Chlair, a word that may relate to wisps or may be an old name for the Kerry or Limerick area (Monaghan, 2004; O hOgain, 2006). On midsummer clumps of straw would be lit on her hill and then scattered through the cultivated fields and cows to propitiate Áine's blessing (O hOgain, 2006). In Áine's story we see a pattern of a Goddess who was demoted to a fairy queen and then a mortal girl in local belief but who continued to be honored nonetheless. The belief in her physical presence and interaction with humans was strong and she is said to be the progenitor of several Irish families.

17. The portions of the original prayer, found in The Year in Ireland, on which this version is based are:

> Love to Thee, O Lord, glory and thanksgiving for this meal and every meal which Thou hast ever given us!...May we be seven times better off at the end of the year, in the greatest graces and the smallest sins! Health of soul and body in people, and their cattle safe from accident, from the year's hardship, from fever and diseases...(Danaher, 1972, p 21).

This prayer was said during the Imbolc celebration, after a girl representing Brigid was invited in, before eating and before weaving the new Brigid's crosses.

18. Traditionally the four treasures are the cauldron of the Dagda, sword of Nuada, spear of Lugh, and the Lia Fal who has no set owner being the stone of sovereignty; however, Young renames them and gives some of them new owners attributing the Sword of Light to Ogma, the Spear of Victory to Nuada, the Cauldron of Plenty to the Dagda, and

the Stone of Destiny to 'Midyir' (properly Midhir). She also assigned directions to each treasure and each city the treasure was brought from which are absent in the older folklore. In the original material, which can be found in the *Lebor Gabala Erenn* and a story called Tuath De Danand na Set soim, the treasures are the sword, spear, cauldron, and stone and with one exception where the sword and spear and reversed they are divided thusly: sword to Nuada, spear to Lugh, cauldron to Dagda, and stone with no set owner.

19. As with Young, Ellis changes who possesses each treasure and even more radically changes the names of each one. He keeps the Stone of Destiny without an owner, as it is in original mythology, and gives the cauldron of plenty to the Dagda. However, he names the spear the 'Red Javelin' and gives it no owner and names the sword 'Retaliator' and gives it to Lugh.

20. The name Boínn is thought to possibly be derived from Bó Fhionn which means 'white cow'.

21. I have drawn this conclusion after a brief survey of neopagan websites and literature, including the Farrar's *The Witches' Goddess*, a variety of books by D J Conway and Edain McCoy and the results of internet searches using the keywords 'Brighid', 'Goddess', and 'Wiccan', as well as personal experiences in the pagan community. This was far from a scientific approach and reflects only my personal opinion based on my observations. In mentioning it within this book I am trying to reflect what seems to be the shifting attitude towards Brigid today, but that shift should not be perceived as judgment.

22. This is based on the idea that families who woke up the morning after Imbolc and found unfavorable omens would offer a black chicken to Brigid to regain her favor. In a modern context chicken could still be offered to her or

could be featured in meals in her honor.

23.　This is modified from an Irish folk charm recorder in the 19th century by Lady Wilde. The original is:

> *If a fairy, or a man, or a woman hath overlooked thee, there are three greater in heaven who will cast all evil from thee into the great and terrible sea. Pray to them, and to the seven angels of God, and they will watch over thee, Amen.* (Wilde, 1991).

I have modified the charm to be more suitable for a pagan audience.

MOON

BOOKS

Moon Books invites you to begin or deepen your encounter with
Paganism, in all its rich, creative, flourishing forms.